SOCIOLOGY OF SCIENCES

GARLAND BIBLIOGRAPHIES
IN SOCIOLOGY
(General editor: Dan A. Chekki)
Vol. 2

GARLAND REFERENCE LIBRARY
OF SOCIAL SCIENCE
Vol. 127

SOCIOLOGY OF SCIENCES
An Annotated Bibliography on
Invisible Colleges, 1972–1981

Daryl E. Chubin

GARLAND PUBLISHING, INC. • NEW YORK & LONDON
1983

Library of Congress Cataloging in Publication Data

Chubin, Daryl E.
  Sociology of sciences.

  (Garland bibliographies in sociology ; v. 2)
(Garland reference library of social science ;
v. 127)
  Includes index.
  1. Communication in science—Social aspects
—Bibliography.   2. Science—Social aspects—
Bibliography.   3. Subject cataloging—
Bibliography. I. Title. II. Series. III. Series:
Garland reference library of social science ;
v. 127.
Z7405.C6C48   1983   [Q223]   016.306'42   82–48773
ISBN 0–8240–9223–6

Printed on acid-free, 250-year-life paper
Manufactured in the United States of America

pl

12-18-84

To
Shirley, Alvin, and Ruth

PREFACE OF THE
GENERAL EDITOR

It is estimated now that there are more than ten million pages of printed matter on science and technology added annually to our collected stock of scientific knowledge. Furthermore, this scientific literature is said to be doubling every six years. In an increasingly complex world, we are being forced to cope with "information overload." New information retrieval and delivery systems are being developed to enable scientists to locate information quickly and effectively.

The communications revolution is already with us. We tend to characterize post-industrial society as the "Information Society." Although modern communication technologies have brought scientists and their ideas together, the increasing delays in publication due to the publication explosion itself have led groups of scientists working in the same specialized area of research to rely more often on informal systems of communication. Informal groups of scientists maintaining frequent exchange of information about their research are known as "research communities," "research networks," "research circles," or "invisible colleges."

The ethos of science includes "communality" as one of its fundamental values and that refers to the principle that knowledge should be shared freely. Increasing growth of the scientific community, increasing specialization, and ever-increasing research output have contributed to the problem of how to get relevant information to the specialist researcher with a minimum of delay. Thus, the emergence of invisible colleges as the centers of advanced basic research in most fields of science has been inevitable.

As the scientific community becomes more and more differentiated, these informal networks and patterns of communication are likely to have a significant impact on the future of science. Although it is unnecessary here to go into the development of the sociology of science, it is relevant to note that it was Derek Price who initially identified the existence and importance of such informal groups and labeled them "invisible colleges." Norman Storer thought of them as custom-made "reference groups." Diana Crane demonstrated how certain types of social organization contribute to the rapid and efficient development of scientific innovations and the diffusion of ideas among scientists. Nicholas Mullins and others have focused their attention on the structure and dynamics of networks or invisible colleges of smaller specialty-oriented groups of scientists.

There has been a growing awareness among scientists that the rapid increase in the rate of scientific literature is a major hurdle to effective communication. In recent years, sociologists and scholars from other disciplines have begun to look into the nature and functions of these invisible colleges and the factors which influence the patterns, speed, and consequences of communication among scientists.

During the past decade, as this volume bears testimony, the most systematic and important research effort in the sociology of sciences has dealt with the networks of communication and social relationships among scientists working in specialized fields.

As a result of the emergence of national science policies in the developed as well as in developing countries, there has been greater recognition of the importance of the comparative framework for the sociological study of science. As a consequence, there have been increasing numbers of studies dealing with the various aspects of science policy and science organization in selected fields in one or more countries.

Today it is rather difficult to limit the sociology of science to any specific discipline because, in addition to sociologists, there are social historians, political scientists, psychologists, philosophers, natural scientists, mathematicians, information scientists, and bibliometricians who have made important contributions to the various branches of this study. Their differences are those of emphasis only.

Grounded on the assumption that all of science is community

based, the study of scientific specialties is a microcosm of the programmatic theoretical and methodological tendencies that pervade science studies. Researchers have adopted a series of concepts to discuss the elusive and complex phenomenon of specialties. These research circles or invisible colleges happen to be international, national, and regional, at times with overlapping members, and differ in visibility and collegiality. As specialization tends to fractionate scientific literatures into even smaller slices, specialty studies seem to be burgeoning. Despite advances in information technologies, retrieving them still remains a challenge.

Daryl Chubin identifies three genres of research centering on communication among scientists. His essay chronicles theoretical and methodological developments since 1972, and traces traditions, themes, and recent trends in this specialized literature on specialties. Furthermore, he offers a few personal observations: on networking and building collegial relations within a research circle and on future trends in specialization.

This volume reflects a rapid growth, diversification, shift in emphasis from the sociology of science to social studies of science, and methodological pluralism in the study of scientific specialization. Chubin's overview tries to unify an otherwise fragmented literature. The classification scheme facilitates referencing and makes cross-connections between sections, authors, approaches, etc. He has systematically reviewed the literature and has organized the bibliographic citations according to subspecialties so that they can be very useful in research and/or teaching.

It is hoped that such an "intellectual accounting," as presented in this volume, continues and that this work will stimulate further research in the sociology of sciences.

Dan A. Chekki
University of Winnipeg

CONTENTS

III. AUTHOR INDEX

ACKNOWLEDGMENTS

It has been well over a year since Richard Newman, Executive Editor at Garland, extended a contract inviting me to produce this volume. He did so on a recommendation from Sociology Editor Dan Chekki. I thank them for their confidence and the opportunity to update my longstanding research interest in scientific specialization. I can only hope that my handiwork will spark a similar interest among others in social studies of science.

Speaking autobiographically, the origins of my interest in "specialties" can be traced to Nick Mullins—virtually a minority of one "back then" who took my early writings seriously; to Jim McCartney, who, as editor of *The Sociological Quarterly* in 1975, published my review article on specialties a year later; and to my "Cornell buddies," especially Dan Sullivan and Ken Studer, who challenged me to shape and reshape my conceptualizations while we were all immersed in specialty case studies of our own. My intellectual debt ever since to Mike Mulkay and other British sociologists too numerous to mention should be clear.

Finally, the nurturance of several colleagues, friends, and relatives during the time I've labored on this manuscript deserves recognition. Thanks to Stan Carpenter, Terry Connolly, Karin Knorr, Mel Kranzberg, Alan Porter, Sal Restivo, Dave Roessner, and Fred Rossini. Special thanks are due the superwomen-secretaries who, often under duress, produced the draft components of the manuscript: Anita Bryant, Vickie Majors, Judy Rogers, and the irrepressible Jane Holley Wilson. The final typed copy attests to the proficiency of Tawanna Ward. To my wife Vicki and children Rand and Jessica, I offer my always inadequate gratitude and apology for making them indulge what they don't always understand. Let me say it in print for a change: I love you.

D.E.C

SOCIOLOGY OF SCIENCES

I. INTRODUCTION

BEYOND INVISIBLE COLLEGES:

A BIBLIOGRAPHIC ESSAY

"Specialization is the hallmark of modern science."
With these words, I began a "State of the Field" review
of the "scientific specialties" literature in 1976.
In the last five years, that literature, according to
the items compiled for the present volume, has at least
doubled. My impression, having monitored the specialty
and "re-discovered" (in my zeal to be comprehensive)
many items I missed the first time around, is that the
claims contained in the newest segment of the literature far outstrip what we "know" or at least can agree
on. The "we" to whom I refer captures the essence of
this volume: students of science who take as problematic the community producing the science itself.

The "problems" derive in large part from the pluralism of approaches that has flourished in social studies of science (Hargens, 1978; Chubin, 1981). In that
sense alone, this volume is a study within a study,
mirroring a larger "community," a microcosm of the
theories, methods and typically implicit epistemological allegiances that compete within and certainly fragment what is at best a community-as-construct. By
qualifying "community" this way, I acknowledge the problematic character of the beast. I seek to confirm
nothing here. Rather, I begin with a construct--more
accurately, a handful or two named below--and seek
evidence (competing claims, if you prefer) that research communities exist. If you find such a claim
mundane, then the evidence I have amassed on factors
which engender and maintain identifiable collectivities may titillate further. To wit, who belongs to
the community and how do we know? How is their activity linked--an array of causal relationships has been
explored--to other constructs, e.g., the growth, obso-

lescence, revolution, or institutionalization of the community?

In the 300-plus items compiled, classified, indexed, and annotated here, there is evidence only that social scientists (predominantly, not exclusively) are studying research communities. By including such studies, I am claiming that they belong to a genre of research that corresponds to the present title that I (and the publisher) have borrowed. Of course, all of science is community-based so that my criterion for inclusion could be a simple, and simply overwhelming, one! Since that will not do, I've applied other criteria. To enumerate them all would not convince all because at least one criterion is aesthetic and difficult to rationalize, namely, something in the paper "clicked" for me sometime during my deliberations on the topic. Specialization is delimiting: to discard a candidate article for inclusion is to reduce the forest by one so that another tree may emerge a bit from the shadows. My delimitation, however, is also self-serving: it makes my task more manageable. And so, it strikes me, that others who study communities similarly rationalize their choices and research decisions.

No doubt, therefore, the literature I have selected to include, and in 80 percent of the cases, to comment briefly upon, will raise eyebrows and bring both guffaws and cries of outrage from wronged readers and omitted authors alike. Such is the prerogative of the annotator: so long as I've "wronged" and "omitted" responsibly, there's no cause for contrition. If readers/authors "identify" other darker motives in my annotations, I welcome their communication with me. After all, this is what a significant part of science is about. If this volume is no spur to further research (and yes, even a little outrage), then my perception of the problems addressed in the specialties literature has been askew. Oftentimes sensibilities are not offended because incoherence, fragmentation, and scatter preclude perceptions. So much for the pragmatic conscience of this annotator.

A. Crane's Agenda--With Reservations

Thus, with this volume, I return to re-survey a literature restricting my focus to the decade spanning 1972-1981. My principal reason for selecting this origin is that Diana Crane's <u>Invisible Colleges</u>: <u>Diffusion of Knowledge in Scientific Communities</u> was published that year. Not only was her monograph theoretically bold, it was bibliographically resourceful. It set forth an agenda which spawned both emulation and recrimination. In the words of Warren Hagstrom (1973),

> It touches upon some of the problems currently central to the sociology of science: the existence and importance of invisible colleges, Thomas Kuhn's paradigms and revolutions, and the measurement and form of scientific growth.

But reviewer Hagstrom had more than unqualified praise for Crane's approach and analysis. Indeed, he articulated some theoretical and methodological reservations that researchers of specialties henceforth both doggedly pursued and blissfully ignored. To wit:

> The theory presented is simple, too simple in fact. It is argued that the growth of science and of scientific specialties follows the logistic curve because it is a social diffusion process .... It seems to me that these results lend scant support to the notion that scientific growth typically follows the logistic curve. Linear or exponential curves fit most of the graphs (showing number of publications or of authors) just as well.

> Crane fruitfully compares the concept of 'invisible college' with Charles Kadushin's 'social circle' (1968), she

> measures the connectedness of these
> networks, and she suggests that such
> networks are necessary conditions for
> scientific growth.... (but) that weakly
> organized areas may be those studied in
> their very early or late stages or may
> be areas not institutionalized in the
> disciplines in which they belong.
>
> Attempts to create a sociology of
> knowledge that fail to consider the
> micro-organization of culture producers
> are doomed to failure.... (yet) Crane
> presents almost nothing about the intel-
> lectual content or the personalities
> working in (her mathematics specialties
> of) diffusion theory or finite groups.

Hagstrom's reservations were portentous indeed.
Studies of scientific specialties flourished in an
"exploding" literature that outgrew its disciplinary
imprimaturs, e.g., sociology of science, and came to be
known as "social studies of science" (see Spiegel-Roesing , 1977a). The problem with calculating the proportion of this literature that specialty studies represent
is one of identification versus definition. As Woolgar
(1976) demonstrated, one researcher's "identification"
(as in discovery) is another's "definition" (as in ar-
bitrary inclusion or exclusion). I'm not inclined to
wrestle with this problem here, but recognize that it
has promoted (and probably inhibited) a good deal of
work, some of which I "define" as relevant to the task
at hand. So although my impression is that the sheer
number of specialty studies published since 1972 has
outstripped the growth of the "science studies" literature in general, I'll leave the precise calculation of
"doubling times" and "half lives" to the bibliometricians, and indicate how specialty analysts have addressed each of Hagstrom's aforementioned reservations.

B. Researching Invisible Colleges: Intersecting Forerunners and Genres

Hagstrom's first reservation concerns the distribution of artifacts, mainly publications, over time.
The temporal connection of published research on a subject or set of problems has been taken, first by information scientists and now by a more exotic (and I
suspect amorphous) breed called "bibliometricians,"
as indicative of a collectivity producing that research
literature. This genre of research, then, centers on
communication among authors--both that formally signi-
fied through publication and that which occurs infor-
mally in "invisible colleges" (Price, 1963). It is
science as a social system that some forerunners of
bibliometrics sought to characterize (e.g., Menzel,
1966; Garvey and Griffith, 1967 ; Garvey, Lin, and Nelson,
1970; Nelson and Pollack, 1970). This concern inter-
sects with a second genre detailed below which focuses
on "coherent groups" of interacting scientists as opposed to social and statistical categories of communication behavior, e.g., by discipline and age.

A related focus within this artifact-based genre,
however, is the establishment and interpretation of
growth curves per se. Illustrative of this approach
are the various statistical bibliographies of specific
subject literatures, e.g., of nitrogen fixation by plants
(Wilson and Fred, 1935) and of mammology (Anderson and
van Gelder, 1970). According to detractors of this
"S-curve" mentality (Rose, 1967; Studer, 1977), the
"growth" that is being measured may be an artifact of
counting. (A related charge fuels the controversy over
Lotka's Law, see Allison et al., 1979.) This is precisely the criticism leveled at Crane by Gilbert and
Woolgar (1974). They ask, in effect, what is a meaningful slice of the literature? Since specialties, like
specialty literatures, possess no inherent boundary,
they must be defined in relative terms. The shape of
the derived curve, therefore, reflects the criteria by
which publications are included in or excluded from that
specialty. The social structural implication, of course,

is that a few persistent authors will be seen as central to the specialty whereas a larger transient set of authors will "emerge" as peripheral. The danger in such an interpretation is that, if we subscribe to the Matthew effect and the accumulation of advantage (Merton, 1968), the central authors become a prestige-laden core while those on the periphery remain intellectually inconsequential for the subsequent growth of the specialty (see Shils, 1961, for such an interpretation). By resisting over-interpretation of the S-curve, the critics sensitize us to the arbitrariness of one's operationalizations which, though tenable, are to many unconvincing. While such criticism has given rise to a more participant-based approach to specialties (discussed below), it is a sobering reminder that "specialty" is a construct and "membership" in a specialty, based on observer-dependent definitions, may be nothing more than a reification of what (we hope and posit) exists.

This brings us to Hagstrom's second reservation and another genre of specialty research. Cognizant of the slippage between postulated specialties and scientists' behavior, researchers adopted a panoply of concepts to discuss the elusive and complex phenomenon I've called "specialties": social circle, research area, community, cluster, network, problem area, problem domain, cognitive region, invisible college, subdiscipline, subfield, coherent group, paradigm group, theory group, and school of thought. Many of these terms are tied to a theory or a technique; some designate a state in a model of specialty development; others are just efforts to distinguish, connote, or innovate. None has enjoyed widespread usage, i.e., the meaning changes with the discipline and mood of the user. With little conceptual or operational comparability, communication among students of specialties has suffered. This, too, of course, serves a purpose of specialization: we communicate with whom we want by publishing in certain literatures. But for the moment let me seek the conceptual closure which the title of the book surely does not convey. In an effort to transcend the connotations of "invisible college" and

move toward "social circles," I would opt for Kadushin's (1976) refinement of this term: "cultural circles" which attract members on the basis of "cognitive
goals such as science and technology." As Bystryn
(1981) puts it, such circles are characterized by:

> (1) no clear boundaries; (2) indirect
> interaction (not everyone has to
> know everyone else or have contact
> with everyone else); (3)...there is
> no formal leadership; (4) it lacks
> instituted structures or norms (cir-
> cles arise to solve the problems of
> individual members who...have com-
> mon needs and interests); and finally
> (5) because they tend to be pegged
> or drapped around other structures.

Here is a definition less deterministic than
Crane's--especially regarding institutionalization--
and intuitively appealing to a bibliographer like myself who perceives a literature with more "scatter"
than "core." Researchers do run in research circles--
sometimes simultaneously in two or three, often sequentially over the course of a career, frequently
forming new and breaking old circles as they go. Research circles are also cosmopolitan and international,
as well as regional and local. They vary in the extent of their visibility and collegiality to "members"
and "non-members" alike, and are fluid structures in
that no rosters are maintained or inventory of acceptable problems publicized. They are, like other social
systems, systematic and capricious in how they operate,
whether they develop, and what they achieve. They are
also ephemeral and that may be their most intriguing
feature. As David Edge (or was it Mike Mulkay?) ob-
served years ago, "By the time we get to studying a
specialty, it may have done its best work and is no
longer viable." We are left with traces--and our
favorite historiographic, bibliometric, or ethnographic devices--to prove that: "Some scientists once
ran in the same research circle for some very good
reasons. Now let me explain how and why...."

Armed with various devices, the forerunners of
the "research circles" literature sought to measure
the factors that bring scientists together, forge their
self-identification, and lead to our recognition of new
disciplines (Ben-David and Collins, 1966; Ihde, 1969;
Russett, 1970), new problems and advances (Deutsch et
al., 1971), and new levels of aggregation of scientific behavior and artifacts (Price and Beaver, 1966;
Mullins, 1968; Storer and Parsons, 1968).

Of special significance in this "conceptual" genre
is the exploration of a specific communication behavior
--the citation of literature in one's publications--as
providing an unobtrusive link (Parker et al., 1967) between the previous work of others and one's own, between what is systematically "signalled" amidst the
publication "noise" in a specialty (Meadows and O'Connor, 1971), and between scientists' private musings and
their public reports. What are the social norms of citation behavior? How accurately do they convey an author's intentions, evaluations, and intellectual processes? What do citations tell us and what do they
obscure? And finally, is there "life" after citation
analysis (Kaplan, 1965)? For many students of specialties, the reply to the last rhetorical question is affirmative. As the annotations will show, citation
analysis is life (and pique) for many: it is, simultaneously, the panacea and the albatross, the height
of objectivity and the depth of numerology, the wonder
and the scourge, the reality and the phrenology, of
social studies of science.

As for Hagstrom's third reservation about Crane's
indifference to the content of the specialties she stu-
died and the personalities populating them, this same
call is echoed by another reviewer of Invisible Colleges (Bosserman, 1973) and a chorus of European his-
torically and philosophically grounded sociologists;
the call is for a sociology of knowledge approach to
the sciences--natural as well as social. There are
very few sociological forerunners to cite. Those of
note who carried out empirical studies in which the
intellectual and the social were presented in context,

warts and all, were Fisher (1966; 1967), Krantz (1969; 1971), and Swatez (1970). The latter is a benchmark in the sociology of science literature for its focus on a laboratory and a research team led by an eminent scientist. It was a case study before such studies of science became fashionable (at least in North America) and before such a site became au courant.

Insofar as the sociology of knowledge emphasis is concerned, Crane's bibliography of 181 sources is telling. Only a dozen reflect this emphasis, including Kuhn's The Structure of Scientific Revolutions (1962), four philosophical works by Stephen Toulmin, four by British scholars, and three by North Americans. Inspecting the bibiliography of my own review article on specialties (Chubin, 1976) shows that among the pre-'72 citations (n=65), only seven reflect a sociology of knowledge perspective. My purpose is not to dwell on the myopia of two North American sociologists, but to contrast our respectively narrow gazes at specialties with the post-1971 literature annotated in this bibliography, and moreover, framed by the theoretical developments in social studies of sciences during the 70s. These developments are highlighted in the following section.

For now, I hope that the case has been made that the research agenda set forth in Invisible Colleges and the reservations expressed by at least one reviewer of it about future specialty studies have been realized. This volume is a testimony that specialty studies are alive and "being kicked around." Although I like to claim that the lack of consensus is healthy, part of that claim is self-deluding. If authors were not publishing in so many diverse invisible colleges/ research circles, I would not have had to run so vigorously among their archives to collect a portion of the entries here. Indeed, specialization is fractionating literatures into ever-smaller bits; retrieving them--marvelous libraries and information technologies notwithstanding--is a challenge. Most research scientists almost cannot afford the time and resources to be up to the challenge. (Gene Garfield, can you hear me?) Such a situation does not bode well for the production of original research. Most claims to novel knowledge will be modest re-discoveries and re-statements of others' thoughts and findings about which we preserved our ignorance (despite <u>Current Contents</u>).

To summarize our current ignorance and knowledge about scientific specialties, I would say that Hagstrom's reservations have been a ticket to "go beyond" invisible colleges and investigate the philosophical, historical, sociological, and bibliometric accounts of specialty formation, evolution, and absorption/demise. For some, knowledge of a specialty is a strong inference from a circumscribed literature. Such observer-dependent studies typically associate bibliometric characteristics with a social structure: community is a corollary of artifacts. The conceptual genre of specialty studies, however, leaves less of the "community under the curve" to chance. These studies seek to ascertain the linkages among specialists, i.e., they insist that categorical definitions will not suffice; only coherent groups with demonstrable communication ties will do.

Meanwhile, the third emphasis, framed by the sociology of knowledge, may be the most incredulous of all. While considering the first genre a fiction of the analyst and the second a leap of faith uninformed by the content of the science under study, the "cognitive sociologist" reconstructs the minutiae of specialization on a case-by-case basis. Shunning both the quantitative evidence of exponential-logistic growth and the network connectedness of core researchers surrounded by marginal contributors, this third genre researcher depends on the reports of the specialty participants themselves, undertakes on occasion first-hand observation, and draws inspiration from forerunners largely outside of both sociology per se and North American sociologists.

With these three genres of studies firmly entrenched, differences in how to conceptualize and measure specialties abound. These differences extend to the very heart of the enterprise. What is taken by some as a legitimate focus for study and a methodology for executing it becomes a contentious issue for others. One researcher's fiction may be another's fact but I, like others, can cite a body of literature that attests to the "fact" that others share my particular fiction. Such consensual pluralism serves to fragment a growing circle of researchers into ever-shrinking spinoff circles. Their intersection--if we believe the patterns of formal and informal communication that have been discerned--becomes infrequent. A concomitant of spiraling specialization could be a trivialization of knowledge. To students of scientific specialties this concomitant is in full force--quite an accomplishment only a decade since the revival of research sparked by Invisible Colleges.

C. Plan of this Chapter

If my prefatory remarks have been the least bit compelling, then what follows in this introductory chapter should be easier to bear. Nevertheless, there remains a dense forest of science studies which, while not embracing specialties, invisible colleges, or what I've called research circles as a prominent construct or unit of analysis, has nurtured many of which presently will command our focus. Thus, I have divided the remaining introduction into two sections. Each provides an overview in the hope of unifying a fragmented literature. To lend some coherence to the bibliographic entries that have been partially obstructed or altogether imperceptible is one goal. Another is that what works for one reader may not work for plenty of others. Thus, my "cuts" are varied and I hope that some slice will reveal an edge that is eminently usable in research or teaching. There is, however, a tradeoff here. As Gusfield (1978) put it:

> To define an area of study and describe
> its parts and direction provides readers
> with boundaries and channels that create
> needed organization and clarity. But
> boundaries are also cages that lock stu-
> dents into ways of thinking and studying
> that shuts them out from the complex and
> unexpected realities of life. There is
> a form of metaphysical arrogance in the
> process of field-building.

The first section chronicles theoretical developments since 1972 that have informed research on specialties. As in the succeeding sections, my form will
be that of a "bibliographic" essay that traces traditions and themes without paying due respect to the programmatic intricacies of the publications themselves.
The second section comments upon the search procedure
and the resultant classification of the bibliographic
entries. Also noted (and rationalized) are the cog-
nate themes deliberately omitted. Then I describe
my annotative conventions and shorthand, and pay ho-
mage to the related bibliographies on which I've drawn
or subconciously modeled the format employed here.
At the end of this section I offer a few personal observations on networking and building collegial relations within a research circle, and on future trends
in specialization, including the compilation and use
of annotated bibliographies.

The Post-1971 Decade: An Overview of Programmatic
(Theoretical and Methodological) Developments

In her introduction to the massive Spiegel-Roesing
and Price-edited volume Science, Technology, and Society: A Cross-Disciplinary Perspective (1977), Spiegel-Roesing (1977) reviews several "tendencies" in
the literature. Her word choice is significant because tendencies need not be mutually exclusive or
differ along disciplinary lines or, for that matter,
categorize the work of a single author uniformly. As

personal research programs evolve, authors tend to
change, if not their orientation or style, then perhaps their subject focus or methodology.

In surveying the theoretical and methodological
developments in social studies of science since 1972,
I am struck by shifting tendencies among authors.
Sometimes these are subtle shifts which the authors
themselves would disclaim. Rarer still are those pro-
clamations that "historians have invaded sociology"
or "philosophers have attempted historical analysis."
The unspoken rule is that there is a "territorial im-
perative" which must be respected. To violate it may
be permissible, but to claim such forays is tantamount
to "intellectual imperialism." For it is the defen-
siveness of disciplines--replete with institutional
traditions--that rejects such forays. Territoriality
is the preserve of specialized professionalized science. It is the status quo of knowledge, the guardian
of obsolescence, the knee-jerk response to the imminent
threat posed by new, often programmatic, knowledge
claims. Ironically, researchers are the source of
such claims so that, as specialties institutionalize,
their knowledge rigidifies and becomes enveloped by a
core of consensus. Out on the "research front," as
Derek Price would put it, the science is pliable and
the claims are numerous. It is there that the "soft
underbelly of science" (Edge, 1979) can be found.

With the proliferation of specialty studies in
the 1970s, several tendencies have been manifested.
Each sports a "soft underbelly" which is nevertheless
connected to a "hard heart" of literature and identifiable proponent authors. In short, the study of scientific specialties is a microcosm of the programmatic
theoretical and methodological tendencies that pervade
science studies. The circles in which these tendencies
are embedded thus can be distinguished by my reading
of the literature and from personal contact I have had
with various proponents. Both of these data sources
can be considered fairly comprehensive, but not exhaustive,

and therefore, fallible in my selective perceptions.
It should also become apparent that emphasizing differences or similarities are two sides of the same
coin. Everyone claims uniqueness to protect some ter-
ritory. Reviewers like myself defy such boundaries
and audaciously plow through all territories, invaria-
bly "missing," "trivializing," and "aggrandizing" all
they see. But somebody must do the plowing!

Such is the curse of the "outsider," as Merton
(1972) cautioned. Although his essay was atypical
of North American sociology of science in the 70's
(since it dealt with perspectives on knowing), it was
followed by much more doctrinaire work that extolled
the virtures of Kuhnian theory in demographic terms
(Mullins, 1975), defended the Mertonian tradition of
internalist studies of scientists' status and social
structure (Cole and Cole, 1973; Ben-David, 1977, 1978;
Zuckerman, 1977), and credited the accessibility of
large computerized data bases such as the Science
Citation Index with the formidable analytical gains
in testing and quantifying generalizations about scientists' normative behavior (Hargens, 1978). (Elsewhere,
Cole and Zuckerman, 1975, and Gaston, 1980, review
these and other developments in an even more flatter-
ing light.) Perhaps of greatest interest as a commentary on the North American contribution, however,
was Merton's (1977) own "episodic memoir" that includes
an intellectual history of Kuhn and other luminaries
who advanced "research procedures" within social studies of science.

Among the minority of North Americans not enamored
of the Mertonian approach and foci, another small sam-
pling can be cited. Reacting against normative and
status preoccupations were Chubin (1976) and Turner
and Chubin (1979). Krohn (1977) and Gruenberg (1978)
offered reflexive accounts of the movement away from
positivism in science studies, while Overington (1979)
charted rationalistic tendencies. Finally, Restivo
(1981a) asked "What is the epistemological relevance
of the sociology of science?" and outlined three

programs (highlighted below) that provide affirmative, but disparate answers.

In terms of narrowing the gap between the sociology of science and related pursuits, e.g., sociology of knowledge and the history and philosophy of science, it was the European sociology literature that posed challenges and alternatives in theory and method. Initially adopting a more critical stance toward Kuhnian theory as a heuristic were Martins (1972), Lammers (1974), and Weingart (1974). Lammers (1974) sounded the battle cry:

> The poly-paradigmatic character of the social sciences is probably not only a function of the vicissitudes of their study objects and of the deficiencies (or peculiarities) of their methods. It stands to reason that the institutional setting of the social sciences also has something to do with their plurality in paradigmatic assumptions... (T)he multiplicity of social scientific conceptions...guarantees that social sciences will never serve one master.

But the Europeans were by no means univocal. For while Whitley (1972) was lamenting the Mertonian "black box" approach and rallying the troops to look inside at the content of science (Whitley, 1974; 1975; Knorr et al., 1975), Law and French (1974) were calling for an "interpretive" approach that seemed to appeal more to British sociologists (Social Studies of Science, 1976) than to those on the Continent. The differential appeal was clear in the British advocacy of case studies of historical episodes and the predominantly German concern with contemporary science policy and the state. Yet these circles intersect at various points, the most obvious being a common tracing of intellectual heritage to Kuhn. Surely, the post-Kuhnian spirit is omnipresent in this literature, but more for the rhetorical purpose of distancing the research from Merton than due to uncritical acceptance of the "normal-revolutionary science" thesis. Indeed, Mulkay (1976) could have had European cognitive sociology of science in mind when he argued that scientists routinely invoke "vocabularies of justification" in accordance with their interests and audience.

Ron Johnston (1976) took another tack: he proposed a "contextual knowledge model" that "overthrows" the internal-external dichotomy in science. Hence, an Australian at Manchester tried to unite in a single statement the interpretive British "strong programme of the sociology of knowledge" with politically-relevant continental research. Coincidentally or not, what followed was an array of policy-related case studies that exemplified versions of a relativistic epistemology. For example, van den Daele et al. (1977) demonstrated the political direction of scientific development, Gilbert (1978) presented a critique of indicators of scientific growth, and Dolby (1979) reflected on "deviant" science as a temporally and culturally relative definition. Mulkay (1979a) epitomized this consolidation of European research by showing that

> in identifying scientific knowledge
> as epistemologically special, and as
> exempt from sociological analysis,
> sociologists have tended to make two
> basic assumptions...namely, that scien-
> tific theories can be clearly validated
> by successful practical application,
> and that the general theoretical formu-
> lations of science do regularly generate
> such practical applications.... Both
> these assumptions are very doubtful.

Advancing concurrently and in a sharply programmatic manner were the respective works of first the Science Studies Unit at Edinburgh and then the so-called Bath school. Relying explicitly on historical and philosophical themes, Barnes (1974), Law (1975), and Bloor (1976), among others, championed the "strong

programme." The themes, if not anathema to many historians and philosophers, as well as sociologists, certainly made them squirm. Meynell (1977) and Millstone
(1978) assailed the Barnes-Bloor notion that "knowledge"
should not be treated as a category analytically distinct from "accepted belief." Trigg (1978), in review-
ing Knowledge and Social Imagery, concluded that "the
'strong programme' of the sociology of knowledge at-
tacks the basic assumptions of our thought and language." Neve (1980) was more sanguine about the "naturalization of science."

In one of his many statements on the "empirical programme of relativism," Collins (1979) observes:

> [A]ssuming that the sociologist is not
> gifted with prescience ...[to] foresee
> the future content of scientific know-
> ledge better than the scientists, this
> leaves hindsight as the sole judge of
> what constitutes revolutionary activity....

It is such bold assertions that carry the theoretical
and methodological proclivities of the "strong pro-
grammers" into confrontations with critics. Retorts
like the following from Barnes (1980) to a "rationalist" are not uncommon in their purpose or fervor:

> The thesis of the homogeneity of explan-
> ation...insists that scientific judg-
> ments are to be explained causally...
> without any regard for whether the judg-
> ments are favorably or unfavorably eval-
> uated. Why then should I be in the
> slightest degree inclined to revise an
> explanation solely because part of the
> explanation is re-evaluated as rational
> rather than irrational? ... if a scien-
> tific rationalist, for example, had writ-
> ten of the causes of the reception of
> Mendelism, then perhaps Roll-Hansen's
> work might give him (or her) food for

thought....Scientific rationalists
must face the fact that their op-
ponents criticize them, not the natural sciences.

Such iconoclasm is similarly flaunted by yet another research circle that brought its force to bear
on science studies of the '70s: social historians of
science. Employing biography--individual and collec-
tive (McGuire, 1973; Shapin and Thackray, 1974; Wersky,
1978)--and quantitative measurement (Thackray, 1977;
Bud et al., 1978) as tools for fusing the history of
ideas and the history of society, social historians
reconstructed in radical, critical, and refreshing
ways the role of science and scientists in society
(Teich and Young, 1973; MacLeod, 1977; Crosland, 1978;
Oleson and Voss, 1979). Again, this work was enriched
both by the case studies of the sociological relati-
vists and the more structural inquiries of the North
American sociologists. The epistemological assumptions and implications that underlay this intersection
themselves did not go unchallenged by the purists in
history. As Cantor (1976), in a review of Barnes'
Scientific Knowledge and Sociological Theory, allowed:
"(E)ven if he has shown that sociology offers a possible method for interpreting science, this is not equi-
valent to the claim that social forces are the only
factors shaping science or that they alone explain all
science."

What could not be readily accepted or its popu-
larity explained was the impact of Kuhn's The Structure of Scientific Revolutions within social studies
of science. The literature it engendered, especially
the widely read Lakatos and Musgrave (1970) collection,
belied the "largely indifferent" reception it received,
in the words of historian Nathan Reingold, "to the spirit and many of the specifics of Kuhn's viewpoint."
If historians were indifferent, philosophers were
downright hostile (e.g., Shapere, 1971; Scheffler,
1972). But in an exceptional display of disciplinary
ecumenism, Reingold (1980) credits Kuhn and the ensuing

debate over paradigms, rationality, and progress, with fueling "the distinction between those historians of science who resolutely consider their task as primarily the 'exposition and elucidation of substantial aspects of the scientific cultures,' largely for their own sake, and those viewing their specialty as providing basic knowledge for application either by other historians or in such fields as science policy."

With these flowers in bloom in the history of science, the prospect of comparable fruition in philosophical circles arises. In the post-Popperian/Lakatosian philosophy of science, we find the staunchest guardians of scientific rationality and realism. Few, however, received serious consideration in social studies of science in the 1970s (a notable exception was Bhaskar, 1975).

Instead, philosophers such as Toulmin (1977) promoted the convergences between history and philosophy. Elkana (1978) went further in suggesting that the distinction between realism and relativism "is not a logical necessity but a historical situation in western scientific culture.... (E)very problem has a realist and a relativist dimension, and the two views can be, and are actually being held simultaneously." Such hypothesized "two-tier thinking" was small comfort to those wedded to the notion of scientific progress, as Laudan reminded in Progress and Its Problems (1977) and his response to its detractors (1980). What Laudan failed to recognize was the sociological significance of proposing the "research tradition" as the scientist's framework and the philosopher's unit of analysis. As I've noted elsewhere (Chubin, 1981):

> Laudan specifies a mechanism which
> commands a scientist's epistemological
> allegiance even in the face of evidence
> that would dispose of its associate the-
> ory or theories. A research tradition
> perseveres because it is 'neither ex-
> planatory, nor predictive, nor directly

testable.' Rather, it is a rallying-
point much like Kuhn's 'paradigm' that
orients and sustains adherents: 'one's
views about appropriate methods of inquiry are generally compatible with one's
views about the objects of inquiry.'

What I later learned (in preparing this chapter)
was Radnitzky's (1974) anticipation of both Laudan's
formulation of "research traditions" and my radical
sociological interpretation of it. Such a sequential
convergence of thought is symptomatic of what the most
disaffected Popperian and gadfly philosopher of this
period, Paul Feyerabend, warned in Against Method (1975)
and in a reply to its critics (1978)--"professionalized
incompetence." In a similar vein, Feyerabend's counter-
part in sociology, Alvin Gouldner (1975-76) denounced
the "virtuosity of the intelligentsia."

Beyond the methodological anarchists and theoretical pessimists of the 1970's, there were tentative
gropings toward rapprochement of disciplinary perspectives and research circle orthodoxies. As for residual
disciplinary murmurings, two are of special import.
First, the near-subterranean enterprise of the social
psychology of science emerged in the form of a major
empirical study (Mitroff, 1974), a methodological guide
(Mitroff and Kilmann, 1978), and two conscientious attempts to codify the psychology of the scientist in
the science studies literature (Fisch, 1977; Mahoney,
1979). Especially apropos here is the latter review.
In it the author maintains that "since most scientists
today are specialists, their individual behavior may
be differentially related to specific issues within
their own specialty. An adequate model of scientific
behavior cannot therefore presume to offer a global
trait-like summary...it would be futile to offer a
monolithic representation of the 'scientific personality.'"

The second disciplinary murmuring came from
anthropology, or more precisely, in an embrace of the

anthropological commitment to in situ analysis. The
social historian of biology, June Goodfield (1977),
emerged from a recombinant DNA laboratory with "a perspective and a plea" that we get closer to both our
subject matter and its producers in their natural habi-
tat. While Geertz (1980) lent both eloquence and the
appropriate disciplinary credibility to this perspective, European sociologists clamored to penetrate the
mysteries of science "in the making". After all, the
essence of interpretive case studies is scientific
practice (Krohn, 1980). Indeed, the so-called social
process of scientific investigation summoned various
ethnographic tools, prominently ethnomethodology and
other elements of the relativistic programs reviewed
above, e.g., discourse analysis (Gilbert and Mulkay,
1980). This generated, again in a programmatic way,
a more subjective, "constructivist" approach to science: how do scientists at work construct and nego-
tiate the reality that is obscured by their written -
and oral accounts?

Finally, we arrive at the evidence for theoretical and methodological rapprochement in social studies
of science. Few works make such overt claims, but the
optimism of their authors can be inferred from a will-
ingness to cite ecumenically and subject the arguments
emanating from different circles to a critical recon-
naissance. Thus, the debut volume of the "Sociology of
Sciences" yearbook (Mendelsohn et al., 1977) illustra-
ted the convergence of philosophical, historical, and
sociological currents in eleven case studies. Other
examples of intersecting circles include Restivo's
(1981c) edited collection of essays on topics ranging
from laboratory life to citation theories, and his own
(Restivo, 1981c) review and typology of programs in
sociology of science: the "strong" program of Barnes,
Bloor, Collins et al.; evolutionary epistemology (or
the more esoteric "moderate" program) of Campbell
(1974) and meta-inquiry (or the "weak" program) which
claims the "metaphilosophy" of Hooker (1975) and the
"metascience" of Wartofsky (1980) as forerunners of
the analysis of "complete systematic world views"

labeled Mertonian, neo-Marxian, etc. In its current
innovative state, only the weak program of meta-inquiry
would seem the pessimistic alternative in regarding
world views as closed systems virtually immune to competing views. Mulkay's (1979b) endorsement of the strong
program as embracing the most robust epistemology for
fostering empirical insights into science leads to a
similar pessimistic conclusion without calling it that.

Perhaps the most hopeful sign that the theory
and method of non-intersecting circles may yet over-
lap to form new empirical connections is the transla-
tion and editing of Ludwik Fleck's (1979) Genesis and
Development of a Scientific Fact (originally published
in German in 1935). Here, Merton collaborated with
historian Thaddeus Trenn to liberate an essentially
"constructivist" account for English-speaking authors.
In the words of reviewer Barbara Rosenkrantz (1981),
an historian:

> From the grab bag of laboratory life,
> Fleck draws insights that are not always
> logically compatible and that frequently
> scrape only the surface of historical and
> contemporary evidence, but they are none-
> theless redolent of those links that tie
> our time to his.... (T)he editor credits
> Fleck with 'prescience' because first
> Hans Reichenbach and later Thomas Kuhn
> found some of Fleck's formulations con-
> genial to their own....Fleck is better
> appreciated when his own modesty and
> specific objectives are remembered and
> intentions are not ascribed to him that
> diminish his actual achievement.

In a single majestic sweep, many of the dichotomies
that have distinguished the theories and associated
methods borne and promoted by the research circles I,
and others, have discerned in the science studies literature seem blurred in Fleck's monograph: realism-
relativism, internalism-externalism, process-product,

normative-interpretive, descriptive-constructive, so-
cial-intellectual, discovery-justification. This is
not to say that these dichotomous themes (which are
more continuous than discrete anyway) are resolved by
Fleck; they are not. They are, however, sufficiently
employed to provoke a considerable critical response
from those who seldom take notice in more than perfunc-
tory ways of scholarship outside their home circle.
Such parochial behavior is territorially defensive,as
discussed earlier, and therefore safe. It is the act
of the over-specialized (oversocialized?) professional.

The antidote, though not terribly contagious or
effective, is to wade into the literature of an "alien"
circle and loose an outsider's fury. I am heartened
by such offenses, even if they "miss the mark"--the
inevitable insider's retort--because they represent
attempts to surmount the "epistemological self-righteousness" (MacIntyre, 1973) that specialization and
intra-circle consensus breeds. Gieryn's (1981) recent
review is just such an attempt. Though flawed by the
inescapable self-righteousness of a (nominal) Mertonian,
it illustrates how constructive discord in social studies of science promises a long life to specialty studies. Gieryn is dubious of

> constructivists' confidence that labora-
> tory ethnographies or scientific dis-
> course represents a more 'real' grasp
> on science than citations or other bibli-
> ometric data....The bugbear: can sociolo-
> gists' interpretations of accounts or of
> ethnographic data be any more free or
> hidden presuppositions and theoretical
> constructs than interpretations of other
> forms of sociological data?

This is a fundamental question debated in several
of the annotations that follow. If each bibliographic
item is viewed skeptically as part of a genre of knowledge claims, and not dogma, about specialties, then
what they encompass, exaggerate, and omit a priori

will come to the fore as divergent conceptions of science. Thus, whether we "let the journals do the talking," believe that specialties exist only in one's mind, or demand that the phenomenology of scientists' routines be recorded by observers of specialties as well as participants in them, we orient our own work as our reference groups would have it. Trapped by circles, our self-definitions are self-serving and - defeating. Victims of a socially-constructed dich an sich, we choose to run in those research circles. Yet the present bibliographic evidence leads me to doubt we have been running in place.

The Bibliography: Search, Classification and Format, Characteristics, and Uses and Trends

The items that I deemed appropriate for this bibliography were derived from numerous sources. As the previous overview of theoretical and methodological developments in science studies indicated, specialty studies are the product of various research circles and programs, each of which often have their own specialized journals and newsletters. These periodicals, in turn, are typically components of larger disciplinary literatures, though a growing literature on interdisciplinary research processes (discussed later) is one recent exception to the general rule. It behooves me, then, to describe my search procedure, outline my classification scheme and format, summarize the characteristics of the literature in each classified section, and offer a prospectus on uses of and trends in this specialized literature on specialties.

A. Search Procedures

Having maintained a personal card file of sources in science studies, I began my search there. Soon I moved to my reprint/preprint file which exhausted my peculiar biases. It was time to consult other sources, preferably compendia. I found nothing as comprehensive as Dedijer's (1969) edited "bibliography of bibliographies" for the subject and period commanding my interest. So I looked elsewhere. One of the periodic bibliographies compiled by Elisabeth Crawford (1974) and

published in Social Science Information gave me a lead
on the "sociology of the social sciences" literature.
Likewise, Hahn's (1980) bibliography provided guidance
to some of the more obscure works in the quantitative
history of science, and Gaston's (1980) was a check on
my North American sociology coverage. The more I looked,
however, the more narrow and centripetal to a specialty
the bibliographies seemed to become, e.g., announcement
of a forthcoming bibliography and index on bibliometrics, 1874-1959 (Pritchard and Wittig, 1981). I sup-
pose my own purview narrowed accordingly, as a few excellent reference guides to the literature of a specific circle, e.g., Mitcham and Grote's (1979) on technology assessment, were added as a single entry to a
section of the present bibliography.

The three bibliographies that were most valuable
for annotation purposes were the compilations of "Citation Analysis" studies by Institute for Scientific Information researchers (Ivory et al., 1976), of "Studies
of Scientific Disciplines" by the National Science Foundation's Office of Planning and Policy Analysis (1979),
and of "Sociology of Science in the West" by British
sociologist Michael Mulkay (1980). In the NSF document,
a "snowball" technique was used to generate over 450
books and articles dealing with disciplines. More than
one-third of these items are annotated. "The principal criterion for selection of items for annotation was
that the item present data-based information on some
enduring aspect of a disciplinary area." Eleven disciplinary categories were used to present the retrieved
literature. Mulkay's bibliography contains 342 items,
nearly all annotated, largely on the post-1970 literature, and preceded by a lucid narrative on the "emergence of the specialty," "patterns of scientific growth,"
and "the social construction of scientific knowledge."
It is a welcome complement to the present volume.

The final component of my search strategy was a
systematic review of the indexes and contents of fif-
teen journals and two newsletters. These periodicals
were selected for publishing works pertinent to social
studies of science and having been in existence for at
least half of the decade under scrutiny here. These

periodicals in history, information science, management, philosophy, psychology, and sociology, and the first years I reviewed of each through unbound issues in 1981, are as follows:

Academy of Management Review (1976)
American Journal of Sociology (1972)
American Sociological Review (1972)
American Psychologist (1974)
American Sociologist, The (1972)
4S Newsletter (Society for Social
    Studies of Science) (1977)
Harvard Newsletter on Public Conceptions
    of Science (now Science, Technology,
    and Human Values (1974)
History of Science (1972)
Human Development (1972)
Information Storage and Retrieval (now
    Information Processing and Management) (1972)
Isis (1972)
Journal of the American Society for Infor-
    mation Science (1972)
Journal of Documentation (1972)
Minerva (1972)
Philosophy of the Social Sciences (1972)
Science Studies (now Social Studies of
    Science) (1972)
Social Science Information (1972)

In addition, spot checks of the following journals were made: Journal of the History of the Behavioral Sciences, Philosophy of Science, Research in the Sociology of Knowledge, Sciences and Art (an annual), The Sociological Quarterly, and Sociology. I think my search biases are apparent: history, philosophy, and information science are underrepresented relative to sociology. Foreign language journals have been ignored.

B. Classification and Format of Entries

The result of my search procedure is a bibliography of primarily the serial literature. A smattering of unpublished reports (working papers and conference presentations), doctoral dissertations, edited books,

and monographs is included. Of the latter, published
reviews of eighteen major books are cited and excerpted
under the monograph in question. Often two reviews of
the same work appear. These reviews are not counted
among the unique entries in the bibliography and hence
carry a lower case letter after the entry number of its
"parent" work, e.g., G91a.

In all, there are 324 unique entries in the subject classification of the bibliography. They are presented in six substantive sections:

General: Theories, Methods, and Compara-
                        tive Studies of Scientific Spe-
                        cialties

Citation-based: A Reference or Citation Approach
                        to Specialty Definition and/or
                        Analysis

Physical Science: Physics, Astronomy, Chemistry,
                        Geology, and Mathematics Spe-
                        cialties

Biomedical Science: Biological, Biomedical, and
                        Agricultural Specialties

Social Science: History, Philosophy, and any
                        "Self" Study of a Social Science
                        Discipline or Specialty

Lab-centered: A Laboratory Site or Local Organ-
                        ization Focus Defines the Analysis

     Each entry is classified into a section based on
its primary focus (as best I could ascertain). In 48
cases, the entry appears in one other section where
the "secondary" focus is of primary interest, e.g., a
co-citation study of collagen is cross-listed under
"Citation-based" and "Biomedical Science." I attempted
neither finer distinctions nor multiple cross-listings
which, in my experience, tend to become more redundant
and cumbersome than helpful.

     If an entry is annotated, the annotation appears
in a block paragraph beneath it. There are 261 annotated entries (80 percent, not counting book reviews),

varying from terse sentence fragments to lengthy comments on strengths, weaknesses, excesses, and related works by the author him/herself or others. Such cross-references use the section letters and numbers (within brackets) unique to this bibliography. Annotations are not duplicated, just author's name and year of the entry. Any material within quotation marks in the annotation refers to the source entry (from the author's abstract or text) unless otherwise noted. In some cases, I have borrowed the annotation, or a part thereof, from one of the three compilations mentioned above. These sources are acknowledged as (I) for Ivory et al./ ISI, (P) for Planning and Policy Analysis/NSF, and (M) for Mulkay. Frequently, my own brief (and dissenting) annotation follows the one cited. Exchanges between authors and critics are arranged sequentially; each has been assigned a unique number followed by an asterisk (*). Finally, an author index, arranged alphabetically, appears at the end of the six subject classifications. Next to the name of each author--there are 284--are the unique section numbers for all entries which list the person as an author or coauthor.

C. Summary Characteristics

The entries, taken by section and collectively as a bibliography on specialty studies, speak for themselves. Because the annotations by myself and others have been incorporated to convey certain information and evaluation, I offer the briefest of summaries. Table 1 cross-tabulates the six subject classifications by five variables: (a) the number of unique entries, (b) the number of entries that appear elsewhere in the classification scheme as primary, (c) the total number of entries [(a) + (b)], (d) the proportion of unique entries that have been annotated (in %), and (c) the proportion of the 1972-81 literature (n=324) represented by the 1979-81 entries (n=125 or 38.6%).

Of interest in this summary table is the comparatively small (n=36) of Citation-based studies. This more accurately reflects the quirks of this bibliographer who assigned 26 entries a primary status in one of the five other sections. Note in column (d) that almost all 36 unique Citation-based entries have been annotated. This contrasts with the proportion annotated in all other non-general sections, which hovers around 75 percent. Column (e) is a crude measure of the recent growth of each subject relative to the others during the last three years. A caveat here is that 1981 is an under-enumerated year: my search was completed in August.

This under-enumeration is also evident in Figure 1. A modest step occurs from 1975 to '76 and a steeper one from 1978 to '79. This becomes the down slope of a three-quartered 1981. For the inveterate "S-curvers," Figure 2 presents the cumulative frequency distribution for the bibliography. Instead of a logistic or decaying exponential curve, we see linear growth with a bump in 1979. I'll forego the second-guessing about "missing" entries (Was I too restrictive, conservative, or uninformed of relevant literature?) and move to a concluding discussion of possible uses for and meanings of what is here.

D. Uses and Trends: Will the Circles be Unbroken?

Second-guessing may be the prerogative of the critic--there's ample evidence in this very bibliography--but second thoughts are an affliction that properly seizes authors, editors, and compilers alike. Without retracting or repudiating that which has passed before me and has found its way into these pages, I must consider: What have I done here? In anticipating the critics and the critical users of this bibliography, my second thoughts gravitate to what has received short shrift.

I have applied a definition of scientific specialties that is tantamount to knowledge specialization, to the aggregation of ideas and people which gains coherence over time. This coherence flags our attention; we recognize an entity that can be circumscribed

Table 1
Summary Characteristics of the
Specialty Studies Classified
in this Bibliography, 1972-81

Classification	(a) No. of Unique entries	(b) No of entries appearing elsewhere as primary entry	(c) total no. entries	(d) % of (a) annotated	(e) % of 1979-81 literature
General	67	--	67	88.1	15.2
Citation-based	36	26	62	94.4	12.0
Physical Science	60	15	75	78.3	17.6
Biomedical Science	57	6	63	73.7	17.6
Social Science	74	1	75	75.7	21.6
Lab-centered	30	--	30	76.7	16.0
All	324	48	361	80.6	38.6

Figure 1

Frequency Distribution of Specialty

Studies by Year, 1972-81

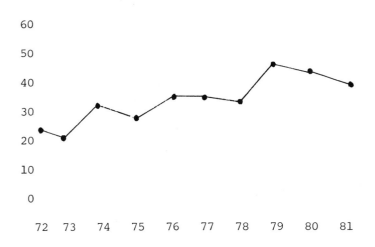

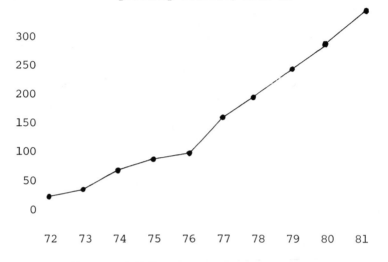

Figure 2

Cumulative Frequency Distribution of

Specialty Studies, 1972-81

as intellectually and socially distinct from others. But specialization is more; it is a claim to expertise, that specialists can provide knowledge which others-- by training, certification, and/or experience--can not. This, of course, is how specialties are professionalized and how specialists within them claim social value, if not indispensability.

Unlike the professions with a lay clientele, e.g., accounting, law, and medicine (Shuchman et al., 1981) scientific specialties relate chiefly to other specialties, other professionals, other experts. If specialization is the key to the economic survival of non-scientific professionals, it may be the key to the social survival of scientists and engineers. For as a science becomes more and more esoteric, its comprehension by the public plummets (Weinberg, 1967). And what the non-scientist or non-specialist fails to understand, he/she begins to doubt and fear (Nelkin, 1978; Ravetz, 1977), as recent debates over genetic engineering, nuclear power, and proposed palliatives for dread disease have shown (Markle and Petersen, 1980; Nelkin, 1980).

My point is that scientific specialties as circles of researchers overlook or underplay the interest group behavior which scientists, as members of an imaginary fraternity known as "the scientific community," display. As Buck (1978) reminds us, this old-fashioned "community" is a highly skilled elite in a bureaucratized work force: Who are these people and what do they want? This bibliography cannot begin to answer such pointed questions; it is for this reason that I exhort readers not to seek generalizations from the entries and annotations, but rather to recognize that "who these people are and what they want" depends on who one talks to, what one reads and how one's own professional ideology predisposes acceptance or rejection of one claim, theory, method, or shred of evidence over another.

One's professional ideology is a cultural phenomenon that endows specialists with special privileges. When specialists act in self-interested ways to preserve

their autonomy, expand their privilege, and propagate
their knowledge claims to whomever will listen, they
are acting <u>politically</u>. In the name of objectivity and
expertise, they are asserting temporary hegemony--and
making scientists and non-scientists alike uncomfortable
enough to prepare for the next round.

What is at stake here are sacrosanct research
values invested in future outcomes. But seldom do we
specialists call it that; talk of politics and ethics
in science is still anathema to most--whether we answer
to the title "sociologist," "philosopher," "doctor" or
"professor" (Rainwater and Pittman, 1967; Studer and
Chubin, 1977). We prefer to list "progress" and "truth"
as our most important products (Comroe and Dripps, 1976;
Rescher, 1978).

I prefer that the prospective reader of this bibliography take my errors of omission and commission for what
they are--a manifestation of flawed professional judg-
ment that is value-laden and tinged by the incompetence
that overspecialization entails. I also prefer that
the reader indulge these errors in the spirit that, to
return to the forest metaphor I applied at the outset
of this chapter, a few trees have been extracted from
the dense forest of "social studies of science." The
trees are "specialty studies." In removing a few of
them from their natural environment, I've necessarily
reduced the forest to a residual significance.

I can only rectify the artificiality of my pur-
posive bibliographic "cuts" now by acknowledging some
other trees which have received short or no shrift.
One is "science policy." I would be naive (I hope) to
think that specialty studies have not been used in the
formulation of policies on research and training priori-
ties. The patrons of science, especially national
governments, have the power and resources to affect the
amount and kinds of inquiry of scientists and other
producers of culture, for that matter (e.g., Ben-David,
1971; Forman, 1974; Heirich, 1977; Chubin and Weinstein,
1980).

Related to this under-represented issue here is
the "career patterns" literature which takes both scientists as a specialized labor force in society and
technically differentiated within the institution of
science itself as problematic. While the careers of
intellectual leaders of schools and traditions and the
founders of entire disciplines are central to many of
the present bibliographic entries (Shils, 1972; Westie,
1975), the manpower aspects of cohorts trained at a
particular time in particular fields (e.g., Chubin et
al, 1981; Harmon, 1978; Reskin, 1976) have been omitted. This was in deference to the "group" criterion
I adopted; with very few exceptions, "categories" of
scientists have been omitted.

A third clump of trees that, ironically, is implicit is nearly all the published entries on specialties
are studies of "peer review." After all, it is the
research traditions, theoretical persuasions, and standards of evidence held by referees of submitted manuscripts, plus the vagaries of editors, that determine
what manuscripts reach the light of print and join the
dusty archives for posterity. This review process, or
rather its results--since access to referee reports is
rare--is among the most contentious issues within the
scientific community. If what is being certified as
"new knowledge" through publication is due to factors
other than, or in addition to, the merits of manuscripts,
then perhaps the system requires reform (e.g., Lindsey,
1978). Likewise, if we substitute research proposals
submitted for federal funding as the focus of peer
reviews, we, as well as the guardians of the dole, begin to wonder: How is "peer" defined" What is the
price of "merit?" And when can the public expect a
return on its investment? All of these are legitimate
questions which have only recently engaged the critical
faculties of social scientists (e.g., Cole et al., 1978;
Chubin, 1980).

Taken together, these three literatures on science
policy, career patterns, and peer review form the context
for assessment of and intersection with the literature

on scientific specialties. Only with this broader
perspective in mind will the trees assume their right-
ful place in the science studies forest. Indeed, if
we look closely at the terrain, we will see that where
there are disciplinary clusters, there are also "inter-
disciplines." "The presumption that 'science' is con-
ducted solely within disciplines dominates establishment practices in funding research, publishing findings,
and advancing careers. Unfortunately, this not only
occasions cracks between disciplines, it fails to provide adequate bridges across intellectual and societal
chasms" (Porter et al., 1980). Such cracks in institu-
tionalized science give research its blurred and dynamic aura. Thus, the leading edge of a boundary that
divides two disciplines is often fuzzy. Years ago
Campbell called the phenomenon a "fish scale," while
others (e.g., Lepenies, 1976) have merely lamented
the dearth of contact between disciplines that should
have much in common.

Faithful to the trend that circles seem to fo-
ment, researchers who share an interest in exploring
interdisciplinary research, as a genre of scientific
collaboration and output, have moved toward visibility
and legitimation in predictable ways. They have
held two international conferences (e.g. Barth and Steck,
1979), formed an International Association for the Study
of Interdisciplinary Research, and claim a journal,
Interdisciplinary Science Reviews, which publishes
only papers invited by the editor, Anthony R. Michaelis.
All the social trappings of specialization, in other
words, are present.

Here, then, is a contemporary example of a scientific specialty which emanates from no single discipline, is endemic to no single setting (if anything,
it thrives in nonacademic settings), and is not formally transmitted via a graduate curriculum. Indeed,
specialists in "interdisciplinarity" are converts.
Foremost among their missions is to introduce the
teaching of interdisciplinary communication and collaboration in the university (Birnbaum, 1978; Rossini

and Porter, 1979). If the purpose of this specialty
is to counter the trend toward fragmentation, then its
cause is noble. But the tactics employed thus far indicate that interdisciplinarity, rather than overcoming
parochialism, will become a victim of it. It claims
to be bucking a trend, but may have to pursue its emu-
lative tack if it is to develop and compete for the
mechanisms that sustain modern science: its own journals, associations, meetings, funding programs, and
no doubt, soon-to-be-heralded orthodoxies and heroes.
Were I to volunteer a prognosis on the growth of interdisciplinarity, as a genre of research supported by a
multidisciplinary circle, I would expect its literature to retain its extensive scatter (and the task of
cumulating a bibliography on the specialty to remain
formidable).

Conclusions

As with the theories, methods, and case studies
presently featured, the circle of researchers in interdisciplinarity will be unbroken. Like other specialists, they will continue running, but that is for
others--participants and observers alike--to document
and divulge. In terms of this bibliography, interdisciplinarity is just one more, albeit intriguing, test
case that specialization is synonymous with research
circles. The very processes by which scientists pro-
claim and disclaim knowledge will continue to originate
and be shrouded there. And, in the next decade, those
who remain intrigued will share membership in a research circle consisting of students of scientific specialties. It is to them--their peculiar and privileged
tendencies--that I bequeath this bibliography.

For those about to embark on a review and/or analysis of the entries that follow, I urge you to share
with me the novel uses to which you apply this bibliography. For my own parochial tendencies have doubt-
less blinded me to obvious applications and findings.
Such interaction through literature is what makes invisible colleges visible and research circles open to

new influences. Any sociology of sciences should welcome such interaction, and indeed devise ways of meld-
ing unobtrusive methodologies with participant-centered ones. I'd like nothing more than to discover
new colleagues in distant sciences whose own parochial
intellectual tendencies converge with my own. That
is what interdisciplinarity is all about--complemen-
tary perspectives on mutual research problems that
promote new approaches and collaborative efforts.
Specialization could have no more glorious end.

REFERENCES

Allison, P.D., D. de S. Price, B.C. Griffith, M.J.
Moravcsik, and J.A. Stewart

1976   "Lotka's Law: A problem in its interpreta-
        tion and application." Social Studies of
        Science 6: 269-276.

Anderson, S. and R.G. van Gelder

1970   "The history and status of the literature
        of mammology." Bioscience 20: 949-957.

Barnes, Barry

1974   Scientific Knowledge and Sociological Theory.
        London: Routledge and Kegan Paul.

1980   "On the causal explanation of scientific
        judgment." Social Science Information 19:
        685-695.

Barth, R.T. and R. Steck (eds.)

1979   Interdisciplinary Research Groups: Their
        Management and Organization. Vancouver:
        University of British Columbia.

Ben-David, Joseph

1977   "Organization, social control, and cognitive
        change in science." Pp. 244-265, 321-323
        in J. Ben-David and T.N. Clark (eds.),
        Culture and Its Creators: Essays in Honor
        of Edward Shils. Chicago: University of
        Chicago Press.

1978   "Emergence of national traditions in the
        sociology of science: The United States
        and Great Britain." Pp. 197-218 in J. Gaston

42

(eds.), _Sociology of Science._ San Francisco: Jossey-Bass.

Ben-David, J. and R. Collins

1966   "Social factors in the origins of a new science: The case for psychology." _American Sociological Review_ 31: 451-465.

Bhaskar, R.

1975   _A Realist Theory of Science._ Leeds: Leeds Books.

Birnbaum, P.H.

1978   "Academic contexts of interdisciplinary research." _Educational Administration Quarterly_ 14: 80-97.

Bloor, David

1976   _Knowledge and Social Imagery._ London: Routledge and Kegan Paul.

Bosserman, Phillip

1973   "Review of Crane's _Invisible Colleges._" _American Journal of Sociology_ 79 (July): 180-182.

Buck, Peter

1978   "Images of the scientific 'community': Commentary on papers by Alice Kimball Smith and Dorothy Nelkin." _Newsletter on Science Technology and Human Values_ 24 (June): 45-47.

Bud, Robert F., P. Thomas Carroll, Jeffrey L. Sturchio, and Arnold Thackray

1978 Chemistry in America, 1876-1976: An Historical Application of Science Indicators. A Report to the National Science Foundation: University of Pennsylvania.

Bystryn, Marcia N.

1981 "Variation in artistic circles." The Sociological Quarterly 22 (Winter): 120-132.

Campbell, Donald T.

1974 "Evolutionary epistemology." In P.A. Schipp (ed.), The Philosophy of Karl Popper, Vol. 14-1. LaSalle, Ill.: Open Court.

Cantor, G.N.

1976 "Method in history: For and Against." History of Science 14: 265-276.

Chubin, Daryl E.

1976 "The conceptualization of scientific specialties." The Sociological Quarterly 17 (Autumn): 448-476.

1980 "Competence is not enough: Essay review of Cole et al.'s Peer Review in the National Science Foundation." Contemporary Sociology 9 (March): 204-207.

1981 "Constructing and reconstructing scientific reality: A meta-analysis." International Society for the Sociology of Knowledge Newsletter 7 (May): 22-28.

Chubin, D.E., A.L. Porter, and M.E. Boeckmann

1981 "Career patterns of scientists: A Case for complementary data." American Sociological Review 46 (August): 488-496.

44

Chubin, D.E. and J.A. Weinstein

    1980   "War painters and western science." Chapter 1 in D.E. Chubin, Social Trappings of Knowledge. Unpublished manuscript.

Cole, Jonathan R. and Stephen Cole

    1973   Social Stratification in Science. Chicago: University of Chicago Press.

Cole, J.R. and H. Zuckerman

    1975   "The emergence of a scientific specialty: The self-exemplifying case of the sociology of science." Pp. 139-174 in L.A. Coser (ed.), The Idea of Social Structure: Papers in Honor of Robert K. Merton. New York: Harcourt , Brace.

Cole, Stephen, Leonard Rubin, and Jonathan R. Cole

    1978   Peer Review in the National Science Foundation. Phase One of a Study. Washington, D.C.: National Academy of Science.

Collins, H.M.

    1979   "The investigation of frames of meaning in science: Complementarity and compromise." The Sociological Review 27: 703-718.

Comroe, J.H., and R.D. Dripps

    1976   "Scientific basis for the support of biomedical science." Science 192 (9 April): 105-111.

Crane, Diana

1972   Invisible Colleges: Diffusion of Knowledge
        in Scientific Communities. Chicago: Uni-
        versity of Chicago Press.

Crawford, Elisabeth (comp.)

1974   "The sociology of the social sciences:
        An international bibliography." Social
        Science Information 13: 215-223.

Crosland, M.P.

1978   "Aspects of international scientific col-
        laboration and organization before 1900."
        Pp. 114-125 in E.G. Forbes (ed.), Human
        Implications of Scientific Advance. Edin-
        burgh University Press.

Dedijer, S. (ed.)

1969   An Attempt at a Bibliography of Biblio-
        graphies in the Science of Science. Lund,
        Sweden: Science Policy Center.

Deutsch, K.W., D. Senghass, and J. Platt

1971   "Conditions favoring major advances in
        social sciences." Science 171 (5 February):
        450-459.

Dolby, R.G.A.

1979   "Reflections on deviant science." Pp. 9-
        47 in R. Wallis (ed.), On the Margins of
        Science: The Social Construction of Re-
        jected Knowledge. Staffordshire: Univer-
        sity of Keele.

46

Edge, David O.

    1979   "Quantitative measures of communication in science: A critical review." History of Science 17: 102-134.

Elkana, Yehuda

    1978   "Two-tier thinking: Philosophical realism and historical relativism." Social Studies of Science 8: 309-326

Feyerbend, Paul

    1975   Against Method. London: Verso.

    1978   "From incompetent professionalism to professionalized incompetence: The rise of a new breed of intellectuals." Philosophy of the Social Sciences 8: 37-53.

Fisch, Rudolf

    1977   "Psychology of science." Pp. 227-318 in I. Spiegel-Roesing and D. deS. Price (eds.), Science, Technology and Society: A Cross Disciplinary Perspective. London and Beverly Hills: Sage.

Fisher, C.S.

    1966   "The death of a mathematical theory: A study in the sociology of knowledge." Archive for History of Exact Sciences 3: 137-159.

    1967   "The last invariant theorists." European Journal of Sociology 8: 216-244.

Fleck, Ludwik

    1979   Genesis and Development of a Scientific
             Fact. F. Bradley and T.J. Trenn (trans.),
             T.J. Trenn and R.K. Merton (eds.). Chi-
             cago: University of Chicago Press.

Forman, Paul

    1974   "The financial support and political
             alignment of physicists in Weimar Ger-
             many." Minerva 12: 39-66.

Garvey, Willam D. and Belver C. Griffith

    1967   "Scientific communication as a social
             system." Science 157 (1 September): 1011-
             1016.

Garvey, W.D., N. Lin, and C.E. Nelson

    1970   "Communication in the physical and social
             sciences." Science 180 (11 December):
             1166-1173.

Gaston, Jerry

    1980   "Sociology of science and technology."
             Pp. 465-526 in P.T. Durbin (ed.), A Guide
             to the Culture of Science, Technology,
             and Medicine. New York: Free Press.

Geertz, Clifford

    1980   "Blurred genres: The refiguration of
             social thought." American Scholar 56
             (Spring): 165-179.

Gieryn, T.F.

    1981   "Relativist/constructivist programs in
             the sociology of science: Redundance and

retreat." Presented at Conference on Epistemologically Relevant Internalist Sociology of Science, Cazenovia, NY (June).

Gilbert, G.N.

1978   "Measuring the growth of science: A review of indicators of scientific growth." Scientometrics 1:9-34.

Gilbert, G.N. and M.J. Mulkay

1980   "Contexts of scientific discourse: Social accounting in experimental papers." Pp. 269-294 in K.D. Knorr et al. (eds.), The Social Process of Scientific Investigation. Dordrecht and Boston: D.Reidel.

Gilbert, G.N. and S. Woolgar

1974   "The quantitative study of science: An examination of the literature." Science Studies 4: 279-294.

Goodfield, June

1977   "Humanity in science: A perspective and a plea." Science 198 (11 November): 580-585.

Gouldner, Alvin W.

1975-76 "Prologue to a theory of revolutionary intellectuals." Telos 26 (Winter): 3-36.

Gruenberg, Barry

1978   "The problem of reflexivity in the sociology of science." Philosophy of the Social Sciences 8 (December): 321-343.

Hagstrom, Warren O.

1973   "Review of Crane's Invisible Colleges."
    Contemporary Sociology 2 (July): 381-383.

Hahn, Roger

1980   A Bibliography of Quantitative Studies
    on Science and Its History. Berkeley
    Papers in History of Science III.

Hargens, Lowell

1978   "Theory and method in the sociology of
    science." Pp. 121-139 in J. Gaston (ed.),
    Sociology of Science. San Francisco:
    Jossey-Bass.

Harmon, Lindsey R.

1978   A Century of Doctorates: Data Analyses
    of Growth and Change. Washington, D.C.:
    National Academy of Sciences.

Heirich, M.

1977   "Why we avoid the key questions: How
    shifts in funding of scientific inquiries
    affect decision-making about science."
    Pp. 234-260 in S. Stich and D. Jackson
    (eds.), The Recombinant DNA Debate. Ann
    Arbor: University of Michigan Press.

Hooker, Clifford A.

1975   "Philosophy and meta-philosophy of science:
    Empiricism, Popperianism and realism."
    Synthese 32: 177-231.

Ihde, A.J.

1969   "An inquiry into the origins of hybrid

50

sciences: Astrophysics and biochemistry."
Journal of Chemical Education 46 (April):
193-196.

Ivory, M.J., J. La Porte, H.G. Small, and J. Stanley

1976   Citation-Analysis: An Annotated Bibliography. Philadelphia: Institute for Scientific Information.

Johnston, Ron

1976   "Contextual knowledge: A model for the
overthrow of the internal/external dichotomy in science." Australian and New Zea-
land Journal of Sociology 12 (October):
193-203.

Kadushin, C.

1968   "Power, influence and social circles: A
new methodology for studying opinion ma-
kers." American Sociological Review 33:
685-699.

1976   "Networks and circles in the production of
culture." Pp. 107-122 in R.A. Peterson (ed.),
The Production of Culture. Beverly Hills:
Sage.

Kaplan, Norman

1965   "The norms of citation behavior: Prolego-
mena to the footnote." American Documentation 16: 179-184.

Knorr, Karin D., Hermann Strasser, and Hans G. Zilian
(eds.)

1975   Determinants and Controls of Scientific
Development. Dordrecht: D. Reidel.

Krantz, D.L. (ed.)

1969   Schools of Psychology. New York: Apple-
ton Century-Crofts.

1971   "The separate worlds of operant and

non-operant psychology." Journal of
Applied Behavioral Analysis 4: 61-70.

Krohn, Roger

    1977   "Scientific ideology and scientific pro-
                cess: The natural history of a conceptual
                shift." Pp. 69-99 in E. Mendelsohn et
                al. (eds.), The Social Production of Sci-
                entific Knowledge. Dordrecht and Boston:
                D. Reidel.

    1980   "Introduction: Toward the empirical stu-
                dy of scientific practice." Pp.xxi-xxv
                in K.D. Knorr et al. (eds.), The Social
                Process of Scientific Investigation.
                Dordrecht and Boston: D.Reidel

Kuhn, Thomas S.

    1962   The Structure of Scientific Revolutions.
                Chicago: University of Chicago Press.

Lakatos, I. and A. Musgrave (eds.)

    1970   Criticism and the Growth of Knowledge.
                Cambridge: Cambridge University Press.

Lammers, Cornelis J.

    1974   "Mono- and poly-paradigmatic developments
                in natural and social sciences." Pp. 123-
                147 in R. Whitley (ed.), Social Processes
                of Scientific Development. London: Rout-
                ledge and Kegan Paul.

Laudan, Larry

    1977   Progress and Its Problems. Berkeley:
                University of California Press.

    1980   "Views of progress: Separating the pil-
                grims from the rakes." Philosophy of
                the Social Sciences 10: 273-286.

52

Law, John

    1975   "Is epistemology redundant? A sociolo-
                gical view." Philosophy of the Social
                Sciences 5: 317-337.

Law, J. and D. French

    1974   "Normative and interpretive sociologies
                of science." Sociological Review 22:
                581-595.

Lepenies, Wolf

    1976   "History and anthropology: A historical
                appraisal of the current contact between
                the disciplines." Social Science Infor-
                mation 15: 287-306.

Lindsey, Duncan

    1978   The Scientific Publication System in the
                Social Sciences. San Francisco: Jossey-
                Bass.

MacIntyre, Alasdair

    1973   "Ideology, social science and revolution."
                Comparative Politics 5 (April).

MacLeod, Roy

    1977   "Changing perspectives in the social
                history of science." Pp. 149-195 in
                I. Spiegel-Roesing and D. de S. Price
                (eds.), Science, Technology, and Society:
                A Cross-Disciplinary Perspective. Beverly
                Hills: Sage.

Mahoney, Michael J.

    1979   "Psychology of the scientist: An evaluative

review." Social Studies of Science 9
(August): 349-375.

Markle, Gerald E. and James C. Petersen (eds.)

1980   Politics, Science, and Cancer: The
Laetrile Phenomenon. Boulder, Colorado:
Westview.

Martins, Herminio

1972   "The Kuhnian 'revolution' and its implications for sociology." Pp. 13-58 in
T.J. Nossiter et al. (eds.), Imagination
and Precision in the Social Sciences.
London: Faber and Faber.

McGuire, J.E.

1973   "Newton and the demonic furies: Some
current problems and approaches in the
history of science." History of Science
11: 21-48.

Meadows, A.J. and J.G. O'Connor

1971   "Bibliographic statistics as a guide to
growth points in science." Science Studies 1 (January): 95-99.

Mendelsohn, E., P. Weingart, and R. Whitley (eds.)

1977   The Social Production of Scientific
Knowledge. Dordrecht: D. Reidel.

Menzel, H.

1966   "Scientific communications: Five social
themes." American Psychologist 21: 999-
1004.

54

Merton, R.K.

    1968   "The Matthew effect in science." Science 159 (5 January): 59-63

    1972   "Insiders and outsiders: A chapter in the sociology of knowledge." American Journal of Sociology 77 (July): 9-47.

    1977   "The sociology of science: An episodic memoir." Pp. 3-141 in R.K. Merton and J. Gaston (eds.), The Sociology of Science in Europe. Carbondale: Southern Illinois University Press.

Meynell, Hugo

    1977   "On the limits of the sociology of knowledge." Social Studies of Science 7: 489-500.

Millstone, Erik

    1978   "A framework for the sociology of knowledge." Social Studies of Science 8: 111-125.

Mitcham, Carl and Jim Grote

    1979   "Technology assessment: Supplementary bibliography." Research in Philosophy and Technology 2: 357-370.

Mitroff, I.I.

    1974   The Subjective Side of Science: A Philosophical Enquiry into the Psychology of the Apollo Moon Scientists. New York: Elsevier.

Mitroff, I.I. and R.H. Kilmann

    1978   Methodological Approaches in the Social Sciences. San Francisco: Jossey-Bass.

Mulkay, Michael

1976   "Norms and ideology in science." Social
           Science Information 15: 637-656.

1979 a   "Knowledge and utility: Implications for
           the sociology of knowledge." Social Stu-
           dies of Science 9 (February): 63-80.

1979 b   Science and the Sociology of Knowledge.
           London: Allen and Unwin.

1980   "Sociology of science in the West."
           Sociology 28 (Winter): Part One (1-116),
           Bibliography (133-184).

Mullins, N.C.

1968   "The distribution of social and cultural
           properties in informal communication net-
           works among biological scientists."
           American Sociological Review 33: 786-797.

1975   "A sociological theory of normal and
           revolutionary science." In K.D. Knorr
           et al. (eds.), Determinants and Control
           of Scientific Development. Boston: Reidel.

Nelkin, Dorothy

1978   "Threats and promises: Negotiating the
           control of research." Daedalus 107
           (Spring): 191-209.

1980   "Science and technology policy and the
           democratic process." Pp. 483-492 in
           The Five-Year Outlook: Problems, Oppor-
           tunities and Constraints in Science and
           Technology. Volume II. Washington, D.
           C.: National Science Foundation.

Nelson, Carnot E. and Donald K. Pollack (eds.)

    1970   Communication among Scientists and Engineers.
            Lexington, Mass.: D.C. Heath.

Neve, Michael

    1980   "The naturalization of science." Social
            Studies of Science 10 (August): 375-391.

Office of Planning and Policy Analysis

    1979   Studies of Scientific Disciplines: An An-
            notated Bibliography. Washington, D.C.:
            National Science Foundation.

Oleson, Alexandra and John Voss (eds.)

    1979   The Organization of Knowledge in Modern
            America, 1860-1920. Baltimore and London:
            Johns Hopkins University Press.

Overington, Michael A.

    1979   "Doing what comes rationally: Some devel-
            opments in metatheory." American Sociolo-
            gist 14 (February): 2-12.

Parker, E.B., W.J. Paisley, and R. Garrett

    1967   Bibliographic Citations as Unobtrusive
            Measures of Scientific Communication.
            Stanford University: Institute for Commu-
            nication Research.

Porter, A.L., F.A. Rossini, D.E. Chubin, and T. Connolly

    1980   "Between disciplines [letter]." Science
            209 (29 August): 966.

Price, Derek deSolla

    1963   Little Science, Big Science. New York
            Columbia University Press.

57

Price, D. deS. and D. deB. Beaver

1966   "Collaboration in an invisible college."
        American Psychologist 2 (November): 1011-
        1018.

Pritchard, Alan with Glenn Wittig

1981   Bibliometrics: A Bibliography and Index,
        Volume 1: 1874-1959. Watford, England:
        ALLM Books.

Radnitzky, Gerard

1974   "Towards a system philosophy of scientific
        research." Philosophy of the Social Sci-
        ences 4: 369-398.

Rainwater, L. and D.J. Pittman

1967   "Ethical problems in studying a politically
        sensitive and deviant community." Social
        Problems 14 (Spring): 357-366.

Ravetz, J.R.

1977   "Criticisms of science." Pp. 71-89 in
        I. Spiegel-Roesing and D. deS. Price (eds.),
        Science, Technology and Society: A Cross-
        Disciplinary Perspective. Beverly Hills:
        Sage.

Reingold, Nathan

1980   "Through paradigm-land to a normal history
        of science." Social Studies of Science
        10 (November): 475-496.

Rescher , Nicholas

1978   Scientific Progress: A Philosophical Essay
        on the Economics of Research in Natural

58

Sciences. Pittsburgh: University of Pittsburg Press.

Reskin, Barbara F.

1976   "Sex differences in status attainment in science: The case of the postdoctoral fellowship." American Sociological Review 41 (August): 597-612.

Restivo, Sal

1981a   "Notes and queries on science, technology, and human values." Science, Technology and Human Values 6 (Winter): 20-24.

1981b   "New Directions in the Sociology of Science." Special Issue of the International Society for Sociology of Knowledge Newsletter 7 (May).

1981c   "Commentary: Some perspectives in contemporary sociology of science." Science, Technology and Human Values 6 (Spring): 22-30.

Rose, Steven

1967   "The S curve considered." Technology and Society 4: 33-39.

Rosenkrantz, Barbara Gutmann

1981   "Reflecktions (Review of Fleck's Genesis and Development of a Scientific Fact)." Isis 72: 96-99.

Rossini, F.A. and A.L. Porter

1979   "Frameworks for integrating interdisciplinary research." Research Policy 8: 70-79.

Russett, B.

1970   "Methodological and theoretical schools

59

in international relations." Pp. 87-105
in N.D. Palmer (ed.), Design for Interna-
tional Relations Research: Scope, Theory
Methods and Relevance. Philadelphia:
American Academy of Political and Social
Science.

Scheffler, I.

1972   "Discussion: Vision and revolution: A
           postscript on Kuhn." Philosophy of Sci-
           ence 39 (September): 366-374.

Shapere, D.

1971   "The paradigm concept." Science 172 (14
           May): 706-709.

Shapin, Steven and Arnold Thackray

1974   "Prosopography as a research tool in his-
           tory of science: The British scientific
           community, 1700-1900." History of Science
           12: 1-28.

Shils, E.

1961   "Centre and periphery." Pp. 117-130 in
           The Logic of Personal Knowledge: Essays
           Presented to Michael Polanyi on his Seven-
           tieth Birthday. London: Routledge.

1972   "Intellectuals, tradition, and the tradi-
           tions of intellectuals: Some preliminary
           considerations." Daedalus 101 (Spring):
           21-34.

Shuchman, Hedvah, Edward Abel, and Susan Frampton

1981   Self-Regulation in the Professions: Ac-
           counting, Law, Medicine. Final Report
           to the National Science Foundation: The

Futures Group.

Social Studies of Science

1976   Special issue: Aspects of the sociology
          of science. 6 (September).

Spiegel-Roesing, Ina

1977a   "Science Studies: Bibliometric and con-
          tent analysis." Social Studies of Sci-
          ence 7 (February): 97-113.

1977b   "The study of science, technology, and
          society (SSTS): Recent trends and future
          challenges." Pp. 7-42 in I. Speigel-Roes-
          ing and D. deS. Price (eds.), Science,
          Technology, and Society: A Cross-Disci-
          plinary Perspective. Beverly Hills: Sage.

Spiegel-Roesing, Ina and D. deS. Price (eds.)

1977   Science, Technology and Society: A Cross-
          Disciplinary Perspective. Beverly Hills:
          Sage.

Storer, N.W. and T. Parsons

1968   "The disciplines as a differentiating
          force." Pp. 101-121 in E.B. Montgomery
          (ed.), The Foundation of Access to Know-
          ledge--A Symposium." Syracuse, N.Y.:
          Division of Summer Sessions, Syracuse
          University.

Studer, K.E.

1977   "Interpreting scientific growth: A com-
          ment on Derek Price's 'Science Since
          Babylon'." History of Science 15: 44-51.

61

Studer, Kenneth E. and D. E. Chubin

1977   "Ethics and the unintended consequences of
        social research: A perspective from the
        sociology of science." Policy Sciences 8:
        111-124.

Swatez, Gerald M.

1970   "The social organization of a university
        laboratory." Minerva 8 (January): 36-58.

Teich, M. and R.M. Young (eds.)

1972   Changing Perspectives in the History of
        Science. London: Heinemann.

Thackray, Arnold

1977   "Measurement in the historiography of sci-
        ence." Pp. 11-30 in Y. Elkana et al. (eds.),
        Toward a Metric Science. New York: Wiley.

Toulmin, Stephen

1977   "From form to function: Philosophy and his-
        tory of science in the 1950s and now."
        Daedalus 106 (Summer): 143-162.

Trigg, Roger

1978   "The sociology of knowledge (Review of
        Bloor's Knowledge and Social Imagery)."
        Philosophy of the Social Sciences 8: 289-298.

Turner, Stephen P. and Daryl E. Chubin

1979   "Chance and eminence in science: Ecclesi-
        astes II." Social Science Information 18:
        437-449.

van den Daele, W., W. Krohn and P. Weingart

    1977   "The political direction of scientific
              development." Pp. 219-242 in E. Mendel-
              sohn et al. (eds.), The Social Production
              of Scientific Knowledge. Sociology of the
              Sciences, Vol.1. Boston and Dordrecht:
              D. Reidel.

Wartofsky, Marx W.

    1980   "The critique of impure reason II: Sin,
              science, and society." Science, Techno-
              logy and Human Values. No. 33 (Fall):
              5-23.

Weinberg, Alvin M.

    1967   Reflections on Big Science. Cambridge,
              Mass.: MIT Press.

Weingart, Peter

    1974   "On a sociological theory of scientific
              change." Pp. 45-68 in R. Whitley (ed.),
              Social Processes of Scientific Development.
              London: Routledge and Kegan Paul.

Wersky, Gary

    1978   The Visible College: The Collective Bio-
              graphy of British Scientific Socialists
              of the 1930s. New York: Holt, Rinehart
              and Winston.

Westie, F.R.

    1973   "Academic expectations for professional
              immortality: A study of legitimation."
              The American Sociologist 8 (February):
              19-32.

Whitley, R.D.

1972   "Black boxism and the sociology of science:
A discussion of the major developments in
the field." Pp. 61-92 in P. Halmos (ed.),
The Sociology of Science. The Sociological
Review Monograph 18 (September).

1974   Social Processes of Scientific Development.
London: Routledge and Kegan Paul.

1975   "Components of scientific activities, their
characteristics and institutionalization in
specialties and research areas." Pp. 37-73
in Knorr K. et al. (eds.), Determinants and
Controls of Scientific Development. Dordrecht: Reidel.

Wilson, D.P. and E.B. Fred

1935   "The growth curve of a scientific literature: Nitrogen fixation by plants." Scientific Monthly 41 (September): 240-250.

Woolgar, S.W.

1976   "The identification and definition of scientific collectivities." Pp. 233-245 In
Gerard Lemaine et al. (eds.), Perspectives
on the Emergence of Scientific Disciplines.
Chicago: Aldine.

Zuckerman, Harriet A.

1977   Scientific Elite: Nobel Laureates in the
United States. New York: Free Press.

II. SUBJECT CLASSIFICATION

GENERAL: Theories, Methods, and Comparative Studies of
        Scientific Specialties

G01. Crane, Diana

      1972 Invisible Colleges: Diffusion of Knowledge
            in Scientific Communities. Chicago: Uni-
            versity of Chicago Presss.

G01a. Bosserman, Phillip

      1973 (Review). American Journal of Sociology
            79 (July): 180-182.

G01b. Hagstrom, Warren O.

      1973 (Review). Contemporary Sociology 2 (July):
            381-383.

G02. Griffith, B.C. and N.C. Mullins

      1972 "Coherent Social Groups in Scientific
            Change." Science 177 (15 September): 959-
            964.
            "Studies six 'small, coherent activist
            groups that had major impacts on their home
            disciplines. . . .' The groups in quantum
            physics, algebra and audition research are
            described as 'elite': divergent but recog-
            nized as central to the discipline. Groups
            in phage biology, operant conditioning, and
            ethnomethodology are 'revolutionary': in
            opposition to a better established group
            or discipline. The groups are characterized
            by high levels of organization and commu-
            nication, identifiable intellectual and
            organizational leaders, and association
            with a particular location"[P].

66

G03.   Krauze, Tadeusz K.

         1972   "Social and Intellectual Structures of
                 Science--A Mathematical Analysis." Social
                 Studies of Science 2: 369-378.
                 "Connections between specialties within
                 one discipline can be represented as pro-
                 ximities and the specialties 'mapped' by
                 multi-dimensional scaling methods. . ."[I].

G04.   McGinnis, R. and V.P. Singh

         1972   "Mobility Patterns in Th₁ e Scientific
                 Disciplines." Presented at Annual Meeting,
                 American Sociological Association (August).
                 One-third of a U.S.-employed sample of phy-
                 sicists, mathematicians, and chemists changed
                 their subfield of research between 1960 and
                 1966.

G05.   Mulkay, M.J.

         1972   The Social Process of Innovation. London:
                 Macmillan.
                 An essay on specialty groups as the social
                 locus of "technical and cognitive norms."

G06.   Mulkay, M.J.

         1972   "Conformity and Innovation in Science."
                 Pp. 5-23 in P. Holmes (ed.), The Sociology
                 of Science. The Sociological Review Mono-
                 graph 18.
                 "[W]hat counts as an interesting problem
                 and as a legitimate solution varies from
                 one specialty to another and within the
                 same specialty over time." The author of-
                 fers a typology of scientific innovations.

G07.   Storer, Norman

         1972   "Relations Among Scientific Disciplines."

Pp. 229-269 in S.Z. Nagi and R.G. Corwin
(eds.), The Social Contexts of Research.
London: Wiley.
"Suggests that relations among scientific
disciplines are indicators of 'the internal
dynamics of scientific enterprise.' Examines
differences between the 'hard' and 'soft'
sciences, between basic and applied research,
and discusses the effect of these differences on professional recognition. Characteristics of disciplines are compared, and
the differences discussed include: demographic differences, occupational differences,
economic differences, 'psychological' differences, organizational differences. Discusses cooperation and competition among
disciplines" [P]. A conceptual forerunner
of much research on subdisciplinary units
of analysis.

G08. Yellin, Joel

1972 "A Model for Research Problem Allocation
Among Members of a Scientific Community."
Journal of Mathematical Sociology 2 (January): 1-36.
An interesting attempt, albeit narrowly
Kuhnified-Mertonized, to model "the time
dependence and dynamics of the allocation
of research problems . . . abstracted from
observation of the high energy physics community."

G09. Zuckerman, Harriet A.

1972 "Interviewing an Ultra-Elite." Public
Opinion Quarterly 36 (Summer):159-175.
The author discusses the challenges facing
a sociologist interviewing Nobel laureates.

G10. van Rossum, W.

> 1973 "Informal Communication and Development of Scientific Fields." Social Science Information 12:63-75.
> The author's thesis is that "when various scientific fields are differentially structured by informal social contacts, the process of dissonance reduction as it relates to the cognitive activities of scientists will lead to a differential development of scientific fields."

G11. Gilbert, G.N. and S. Woolgar

> 1974 "The Quantitative Study of Science: An Examination of the Literature." Science Studies 4:279-294.
> A critique of Crane [G01] and literature-based approaches to scientific growth.

G12. Mulkay, M.J.

> 1974 "Methodology in the Sociology of Science: Some Reflections on the Study of Radio Astronomy." Social Science Information 13:107-119.
> The author warns of scientists' "implicit theory of citing"; he also extols the virtues of a sociologist's collaboration with a scientist-insider, especially when interviewing scientists about the content of their research.

G13. Mulkay, M.J.

> 1974 "Conceptual Displacement and Migration in Science: A Prefatory Paper." Science Studies 4:205-234.
> "Studies the movement of scientists from one research area to another, and examines the corresponding changes in social

relationships and research activities
(how skills and concepts are applied in
new fields). Discusses five individual
cases (solar physics to zoology; physics
to radar meteor astronomy to geophysics;
radar meteor astronomy to glaciology;
zoology to psychology; engineering to bio-
engineering)" [P].

G14. Small, H. and B.C. Griffith

1974 "The Structure of Scientific Literatures
I: Identifying and Graphing Specialties."
Science Studies 4:17-40.
"Reports on techniques for identifying
clusters of highly interactive documents
in science (co-citation analysis). This
technique opens the way to a systematic
exploration of the specialty structure of
science, including both the internal structure of specialties and their relationship
to one another. Examines in some detail
clusters in nuclear physics, particles
physics and biomedicine" [P].

G15. Vlachy, Jan

1974 "Distribution Patterns in Creative Communities." Presented at Eight World Congress
of Sociology, Toronto (August).
Over 500 professional creative populations
in the sciences, arts, music, and theater
are related to the distribution patterns
of their respective artifacts, including
publications, letters, musical compositions,
paintings, and sculptures.

G16. Whitley, R.D.

1974 Cognitive and Social Institutionalization
of Scientific Specialties and Research
Areas." Pp. 69-95 in Richard D. Whitley

(ed.), Social Processes of Scientific Development. London: Routledge and Kegan Paul. "While at the specialty level, cognitive development will consist largely of reformulating and articulating different models and their implications for understanding some aspect of reality, at the research area level . . . two alternative modes of development may take place. . . . [I]n specialties and research areas which have a low degree of cognitive and social institutionalization, a myriad of ideas and data are produced by very small collectivities which are not connected and not necessarily consistent over time. The area will probably be continuously redefined as interests change. . . ."

G17. Boehme, Gernot

1975 "The Social Function of Cognitive Structures: A Concept of the Scientific Community within a Theory of Action." Pp. 205-225 in K.D. Knorr et al. (eds.), Determinants and Controls of Scientific Development. Boston: Reidel.
The author exhorts sociologists to study the "structure of argumentation" of scientists.

G18. Bourdieu, Pierre

1975 "The Specificity of the Scientific Field and the Social Conditions of the Progress of Reasons." Social Science Information 14:19-47.
"[T]he scientific field is the locus of a competitive struggle in which the specific issue at stake is the monopoly of scientific authority, defined inseparably as technical capacity and social power, or . . . . the monopoly of scientific compe-

tence, in the sense of a particular agent's
socially recognized capacity to speak and
act legitmately . . . in scientific matters."
The author's theory views scientists' "ideological strateqies" as self-justifying.

G19. Chubin, D.E.

1975   "Trusted Assessorship in Science: A Relation
in Need of Data." Social Studies of Science
5 (August): 362-368.
Use of "title-page" acknowledgements as a
measure of informal communication between
authors and "trusted assessors."

G20. Mulkay, M.J.

1975   "Three Models of Scientific Development."
The Sociological Review 23 (August):509-538.
Not one of Mulkay's best (see Law and Barnes
[G21*]).

G21.*Law, J. and B. Barnes

1976   "Areas of Ignorance in Normal Science. A
Note on Mulkay's 'Three Models of Scientific Development.'" Sociological Review 24
(February): 115-124.
The authors argue that Mulkay has made a
false contrast between the models of "branching" and "closure"--that is, between his
own account and that of Kuhn. "The latter,
which reflects an interest in the process
of cultural change, is not necessarily in
conflict with the former, which reflects
rather, an interest in the consequences of
scientific change or innovation and, in
particular, in the social reorganization
that sometimes thereby results."

72

G22.*Mulkay, M.J.

1976   "The Model of Branching." Sociological
Review 24 (February): 125-133.
"Where we differ most is in our interpretation of Kuhn. . .In the model of branching, an attempt was made to use participants' labels and participants' accounts
along with as wide a range as possible of
other empirical material in order to produce
a dynamic analysis of cultural and social
processes in science."

G23. Mulkay, M.J.,G.N. Gilbert, and S. Woolgar

1975   "Problem Areas and Research Networks in
Science." Sociology 9: 187-203.
"Examines the social and intellectual processes involved in emergence, growth and
decline of scientific research networks and
their associated problem areas. Identifies
three phases of development: (1) exploratory
phase, characterized by lack of effective
communication and imprecise definition of
problems; (2) rapid growth phase, characterized by increasing social and intellectual
integration, made possible by improved communication; (3) final phase, characterized
by the decline of the network and the movement of participants to new areas of scientific opportunity" [P]. A British version
of Chubin [G24] that is highly cited on
both sides of the Atlantic

G24. Chubin, Daryl E.

1976   "The Conceptualization of Scientific Specialties." The Sociological Quarterly 17
(Autumn): 448-496.

G25. Lemaine, Gerard, Roy MacLeod, Michael Mulkay, and

Peter Weingart (eds.)

1976 Perspectives on the Emergence of Scientific Disciplines. The Hague and Paris: Mouton-Aldine.

G25a. Chubin, D.E.

1978 (Review). Newsletter of the Society for Social Studies of Science 3 (Summer):27-28.
"This volume is part of the European barrage of collections--this one courtesy of Project PAREX--devoted to scientific innovation, the legitimation of new specialties, and the institutionalization of disciplines. The focus here ranges from agricultural chemistry to tropical medicine and radar meteor research. In all, the collection contains thirteen essays (two in French), four of which were published in 1973-75 in Social Studies of Science or Social Science Information, and some of which have since been superseded by the authors' own longer article or monographic treatments." Especially worthy of attention is the editors' introduction [G26], which suggests that studying the emergence of new disciplines "is minimally a tripartite problem of measuring the rate, direction, and intellectual content of scientific development," and the paper by van den Daele and Weingart [G28].

G26. Lemaine, Gerard, Roy MacLeod, Michael Mulkay, and Peter Weingart

1976 "Problems in the Emergence of New Disciplines." Pp. 1-23 in Lemaine et al. (eds.), [G25].

G27. Robbins, David and Ron Johnston

1976 "The Role of Cognitive and Occupational Differentiation in Scientific Controversies." <u>Social Studies of Science</u> 6: 349-368.
The authors claim "there is a need that analyses of such issues as the basis of conflict between experts, and the relationship between political institutions and the scientific community and its sub-groups, be informed by a conception of scientific knowledge not as absolute or given, but as socially constructed. . . . [T]he possibility is admitted that science is differentiated, to the extent that scientists working within widely separated specialties can on strict scientific grounds reach genuinely opposed conclusions, and that the heat of disputes between experts may be an indication of attempts by competing groups of scientists to establish their professional authority over a particular issue or area." This perspective is applied to the controversies over environmental lead levels, low-level radiation, and the ABM system.

G28. van den Daele, W. and P. Weingart

1976 "Resistance and Receptivity of Science to External Direction: The Emergence of New Disciplines under the Impact of Science Policy." Pp. 247-275 in Lemaine et al. (eds.), [G25].
Research in policy areas such as space, cancer, and environmental studies is conceptualized on three levels: "on the <u>policy</u> level, in which the objectives of science policy must be classified; on the <u>cognitive</u> level, in which the structures of science are defined as a cultural or intellectual

enterprise; and on the institutional level;
in which science is defined in terms of
a system of social action."

G29. Whitley, Richard

   1976   "Umbrella and Polytheistic Scientific Dis-
           ciplines and Their Elites." Social Stu-
           dies of Science 6 (September): 471-497.
           "A distinction is drawn between disciplines
           which act as loose holding organizations
           for diverse specialties and those where
           scientific work is organized around diver-
           gent views of the disciplines" [M].

G30. Woolgar, S.W.

   1976   "The Identification and Definition of
           Scientific Collectivities." Pp. 233-245
           in Lemaine et al. (eds.), [G25].

G31. Woolgar, S.W.

   1976   "Writing an Intellectual History of Scien-
           tific Development: The Use of Discovery
           Accounts." Social Studies of Science 6
           (September): 395-422.
           "A systematic investigation of the range
           of variation in accounts of the discovery
           of pulsars, and of the difficulties in
           using such accounts to provide the basis
           for a 'definitive' sociological version
           of events" [M]. An important demonstra-
           tion of scientists' rhetoric and their
           penchant for creating 'revisionist' his-
           tory (see Mulkay [G12]).

G32. Chubin, D.E., P.T. Carroll, and K.E. Studer

   1977   "Underpinnings and Overselling: A Comment
           upon Two Block-Model Studies of Cocitation
           Clusters." Unpublished paper.

". . . if the purpose of the Breiger [B16]
and the Mullins et al. [B25] analyses is
to demonstrate a link between a retrieved
literature and a socially coherent group
that produced it, then why blockmodel? On
the other hand, if the social coherence of
the group is in question, then why begin
with cocitation clusters? One can hear
drums beating for the two tools, cocitation
and blockmodeling, but what these tools
clarify (i.e., a certain kind of data)
tends to obscure the ultimate understanding
of socially coherent scientific communities." This paper is centrally featured
in Lenoir [B45].

G33. Cole, S., J.R. Cole, and L. Dietrich

1977   "Measuring the Cognitive State of Scientific Disciplines." Pp. 209-251 in Y. Elkana
et al. (eds.), Toward a Metric of Science.
New York: Wiley.
"This paper employs factor analysis of citations, Gini coefficients of citation
distributions, and cocitation matrices to
compare the cognitive structure and consensus in over 30 scientific disciplines
and specialties. . . . The research indicates that whole disciplines can no longer
be considered as meaningful units for study . . ." [I]. What comes as a revelation
to the authors was amply documented--on
the basis of different methods and evi-
dence--a few years earlier.

G34. Dolby, R.G.A.

1977   "The Transmission of Science." History
of Science 15:1-43.
A masterful historical presentation, with
nods to the sociological literature, of
the thesis that "the processes by which

science is transmitted also select and
transform its content."

G35. Edge, D.O.

1977   "Why I Am Not a Co-citationist." Newslet-
ter of the Society for Social Studies of
Science 2 (Summer): 13-19.
An early version of Edge [G51]; its signi-
ficance is discussed in Griffith
[C35] and Morman [G60].

G36. Gilbert, G. Nigel

1977   "Referencing as Persuasion." Social Studies of Science 7: 113-122.
"Research papers are seen as instruments
of persuasion and references are conceived
as aids which are used to increase papers'
persuasive power" [M]. In a theoretical
sense, this paper throws down the gauntlet
to citation analysts.

G37. Griffith, B.C., M.C. Drott, and H.G. Small

1977   "On the Use of Citations in Studying Scientific Achievements and Communication."
Newsletter of the Society for Social Studies of Science 2 (Summer): 9-13.

G38. Johnston, Ron and D. Robbins

1977   "The Development of Specialties in Indus-
trialized Science." Sociological Review
25: 87-108.
An attempt to develop a framework (outlined
in Robbins and Johnston [G27]) for examining
the impact of imposing external goals on
differentiation within science. "Using
the concept of occupational control, conditions of patronage and state mediation"
are shown to promote differentiation and

emergence of new specialties.

G39. Mulkay, M.J.

    1977   "Sociology of the Scientific Research Community." Pp. 93-148 in I. Spiegel-Roesing and D. de S. Price (eds.), Science, Technology and Society: A Cross-Disciplinary Perspective. Beverly Hills: Sage.

G40. Overington, Michael A.

    1977   "The Scientific Community as Audience: Toward a Rhetorical Analysis of Science." Philosophy and Rhetoric 10 (Summer): 143-164.
          A linguistic approach to understanding the social functions of specialized communication.

G41. Pyenson, Lewis and Douglas Skopp

    1977   "Educating Physicists in Germany Circa 1900." Social Studies of Science 7 (August): 329-366.
          A collective biography of physicists in Germany circa 1900, interesting for its historical approach to disciplines: "Historians have recognized that many branches of the modern sciences follow distinct visions of reality and operate within different social settings. . . .Disciplines may be thought of as the different cultures that compose the human enterprise of science. Considering disciplines as different cultures poses three problems for the historian of science. These problems concern disciplinary taxonomy, the temporality of disciplines, and disciplinary patterns of thought."

G42. Sullivan, D., D.H. White, and E.J. Barboni

1977   "Co-citation Analyses of Science: An
        Evaluation." Social Studies of Science
        7 (May): 223-240.
        An endorsement, albeit with qualifica-
        tion, of co-citation analysis as a con-
        firmatory tool for intellectual history,
        at least in the particle physics specialty
        described in [P28].

G43. Friedkin, N.E.

1978   "University Social Structure and Social
        Networks Among Scientists." American
        Journal of Sociology 83: 1444-1465.
        Describes "the pattern of research com-
        munication among faculty in the six phy-
        sical science departments of an elite
        American university . . . and suggests
        that university social structure can
        foster an integrative social network
        which is multidisciplinary in composi-
        tion." An excellent empirical study of
        a "local" network, its elitism notwith-
        standing.

G44. Gieryn, Thomas F.

1978   "Problem Retention and Problem Change."
        Pp. 96-115 in J. Gaston (ed.), The So-
        ciology of Science. San Francisco: Jos-
        sey-Bass.
        The reasons scientists persist in or
        change their research direction is ex-
        plored in the context of contemporary
        American astronomy (based on the author's
        doctoral dissertation, Columbia Universi-
        ty, 1979).

G45. Gieryn, Thomas F. and Robert K. Merton

    1978   "The Sociological Study of Scientific
Specialties." Social Studies of Science
8 (May): 257-261.
An essay review of Edge and Mulkay [P19]
and Lemaine et al. [G25]. "[O]ne theme
comes to a head in these two volumes: a
movement toward increased concern with
the content of scientific knowledge. . . .
[A] major next step is the formulation
of a set of analytical concepts for describing cognitive structures of science
in terms of allowing systematic empirical
investigation."

G46, Small, Henry G.

    1978   "Cited documents as concept symbols."
Social Studies of Science 8 (August): 327-
340.
"In citing a document an author is creat-
ing its meaning, and this [Small argues],
is a process of symbol making." Based on
a textual analysis of a sample of highly
cited documents in chemistry, he finds a
"high degree of uniformity . . . in the
association of specific concepts with specific documents. . . . It is the process
of acquiring a standard of conventional
interpretation that is crucial for the
social determination of scientific ideas."

G47. Social Studies of Science

    1978   Theme Issue: Sociology of Mathematics. 8
(February).
Articles on Karl Pearson, statistics and
social interests, and the value-laden character of game theory.

G48. Zuckerman, H.

    1978   "Theory Choice and Problem Choice in Science." Pp. 65-95 in J. Gaston (ed.), The Sociology of Science. San Francisco: Jossey Bass.
    An internalist, super-rationalist account.

G49. Barnes, Barry and Steven Shapin (eds.).

    1979   Natural Order: Historical Studies of Scientific Culture. Beverly Hills and London: Sage.

G49a. Rosenberg, Charles E.

    1980   "Nature Decoded" (Review). Isis 71 (June): 291-295.
    "[T]his book might itself be understood as an object of the same sort of analysis it prescribes for other cultural artifacts . . . . To deny the transcendence of scientific knowledge is, after all, a political act. The contextual approach to science is a social tool as well as an epistemology . . . for the program which Barnes and Shapin outline with such enthusiasm is forbidding indeed: to recreate the context of ideas, pinpoint the social place of knowledge producers, evaluate the subtle ways in which social perception influences the choice among intellectual options."

G49b. Rudwick, Martin

    1980   "Social Order and the Natural World" (Review). History of Science 18: 269-285.
    [T]he editors' concern to encourage explicit theorizing by historians of science should surely be welcomed. . . . [B]ut above all . . . the relation between

82

'technical interests' and 'social interest'
remains obscure. "

G50. Dolby, R.G.A.

1979   "Reflections on Deviant Science." Pp. 9-
47 in R. Wallis (ed.), On the Margins of
Science: The Social Construction of Rejected Knowledge. Staffordshire: University of Keele.
The author cogently argues that definitions of "pseudo" and real sciences are
temporally and culturally relative. So
must our assessments of them, for "if
fringe groups can occur in our culture
at the present time, which defend deviant
beliefs to their own standards of rationality, are we to dismiss their reasoning
without attempting to understand it, merely
because it seems silly to us?"

G51. Edge, David O.

1979   "Quantitative Measures of Communication
in Science: A Critical Review." History
of Science 17: 102-134.
A forceful discussion which updates Edge
[G25], arguing that "those who adopt these
[quantitative] methods (and in particular,
citation analysis) make implicit assumptions about the nature of science; and,
moreover, that what they gloss over as
unproblematic are precisely the points
which many of us find to be crucially at
issue."

G52. Miller, S.M.

1979   "Circles, Pairs, Schools, Lines, and Mi-
lieux: Notes on Intellectual Work Situa-
tions." Mimeo: Boston University.
A working paper on informal collaborations

and creativity in science.

G53. Nelkin, Dorothy (ed.).

1979   Controversy: Politics of Technical Decisions. Beverly Hills: Sage.
A very readable collection of case studies of technical disputes which have
spilled out of research communities into
the public domain where disciplinary expertise is seen as just another ideology.

G54. Oleson, Alexandra and John Voss (eds.).

1979   The Organization of Knowledge in Modern
America 1860-1920. Baltimore and London:
John Hopkins University Press.
In their introduction to the 17 essays
in this collection, the editors ask, "How
did the modern organization of knowledge
come into being?" The answers to this
and related questions "lie in the interaction of the ideas, individuals, and institutions actively involved in the transformation." Of particular interest to
students of specialization are the essays
by Allen [B37], Rossiter [B47], and Rosenberg [G55].

G55. Rosenberg, Charles

1979   "Toward and Ecology of Knowledge: On Discipline, Context, and History." Pp. 440-
455 in A. Oleson and J. Voss (eds.),
[G55].
A concluding essay on "the cultural revolution that took place in the half-cen-
tury before 1981: the changing nature of
organized knowledge and the contexts in
which it was elaborated, transmitted,
and used.

G56. Wallis, Roy (ed.)

　　　1979　On the Margins of Science: The Social Con-
　　　　　　struction of Rejected Knowledge. Keele,
　　　　　　Staffordshire: University of Keele (Socio-
　　　　　　logical Review Monograph 27).
　　　　　　This collection of thirteen case studies
　　　　　　seeks to demonstrate that the line separat-
　　　　　　ing accepted from rejected knowledge is
　　　　　　fine indeed, perhaps imperceptible. In the
　　　　　　editor's words, a "changing ethos . . .
　　　　　　provokes a re-consideration of the histori-
　　　　　　cal, social and cognitive circumstances
　　　　　　surrounding and embedded in the success or
　　　　　　failure of particular knowledge-claims."
　　　　　　For examples, see Dolby [G50], Webster
　　　　　　[B48], and Collins and Pinch [S49].

G57. Cozzens, Susan E.

　　　1980　"Operationalizing Problems and Problem
　　　　　　Areas." Presented at Fifth Annual Meeting,
　　　　　　Society for Social Studies of Science, To-
　　　　　　ronto (October).
　　　　　　" . . . sociologists need to reach consen-
　　　　　　sus on an acceptable operational definition
　　　　　　of a problem area. In this paper, I re-
　　　　　　view both conceptual and operational defi-
　　　　　　nitions for the terms problem and problem
　　　　　　area." The problem is more that termino-
　　　　　　logical. . . .

G58. Dolby, R.G.A.

　　　1980　"On the Autonomy of Pure Science: The Con-
　　　　　　struction and Maintenance of Barriers be-
　　　　　　tween Scientific Establishments and Popu-
　　　　　　lar Culture." Presented at Conference on
　　　　　　Scientific Establishments and Hierarchies,
　　　　　　Oxford University (July).
　　　　　　Part 2 of Dolby [G50].

G59. Lewis, Gwendolyn L.

1980   "The Relationship of Conceptual Development
        to Consensus: An Exploratory Analysis of
        Three Subfields." Social Studies of Sci-
        ence 10: 285-308.
        "This article reports on a study of the re-
        lationship between conceptual development
        and consensus on research issues in three
        scientific subfields--solid state physics,
        genetics, and developmental psychology."
        Dependence on the phase models of Mulkay
        [G20] and Mullins [B01] and the North Ameri-
        can devotion to quantitative analysis ren-
        der this promising study to be doctrinaire
        sociology of science.

G60. Morman, Edward T.

1980   "Citation Analysis and the Current Debate
        over Quantitative Methods in the Social
        Studies of Science." 4S Newsletter 5 (Sum-
        mer): 7-13.
        "[Eugene Garfield's] view of citation analy-
        sis as objective and thus of 'preferred
        logical status' (Edge [G51] uses this phrase
        disparagingly but not inappropriately) is
        important if only because many science po-
        licy makers tend to agree with it. . . .
        Small and Griffith [G14] explicitly link
        their work to historians and sociologists
        of science and to information scientists
        who regard sub-disciplinary specialties
        as the building blocks of science, and
        who attempt to map them." Morman's dis-
        cussion also includes "an overview of the
        debate" over citation analysis that centers
        on "contrasting traditions which result in
        a clash of professional vested interests,
        and concerns for the use of technical com-
        petencies by both the practitioners and
        opponents of citation analysis." The

essay is a good example of overdue "meta-
analysis" of science (see Chubin [G64]).

G61. Neve, Michael

　1980　"The Naturalization of Science." Social
　　　　Studies of Science 10 (August): 375-391.

　　　　An essay review of three formidable collec-
　　　　tions--Barnes and Shapin [G49], Jordanova
　　　　and Porter [B42], and Wallis [G56].

G62. Woolgar, Steve

　1980　"Discovery: Logic and Sequence in a Scien-
　　　　tific Text." Pp. 239-268 in K. Knorr, R.
　　　　Krohn, and R.D. Whitley (eds.), The Social
　　　　Process of Scientific Investigation. So-
　　　　ciology of the Sciences, Vol. 4. Boston:
　　　　Reidel.
　　　　"An analytic perspective informed by ethno-
　　　　methodological thinking is located in re-
　　　　lation to the debate between rationalist
　　　　philosophy and the strong programme in the
　　　　sociology of knowledge. This debate is
　　　　taken as the basis for an examination . . .
　　　　of isomorphism between presentational con-
　　　　text and scientific concepts. The second
　　　　part of this paper offers a tentative analy-
　　　　sis of one aspect of the practical activi-
　　　　ty of scientific investigation: the accom-
　　　　plishment of a discovery as related in a
　　　　scientific text." This is a most accessi-
　　　　ble example of ethnomethodology applied
　　　　to science.

G63. Ziman, John

　1980　"What are the Options?" Social Determinants
　　　　of Personal Research Plans." Presented at
　　　　the Conference on Scientific Establishments
　　　　and Hierarchies, Oxford University (June).

This long essay asks, "To what range of
'realistic' possibilities do scientists
restrict themselves when they consciously
consider their research objectives? This
question involves so many intangible and
idiosyncratic factors that it can only be
posed schematically: yet it touches upon
a crucial point . . . the means by which
individual scientists are kept, at least
to some extent, under social control." In
this expanded version, the author discusses the communal yet local influences on
the formulation and execution of personal
research programs in his inimitable blend
of folk wisdom and keen insight. The 170-
item bibliography is a bonus for the over-
specialized reader.

G64. Chubin, Daryl E.

1981   "Constructing and Reconstructing Scienti-
        fic Reality: A Meta-analysis." Interna-
        tional Society for the Sociology of Know-
        ledge Newsletter 7 (May): 22-28.
        After introducing the notion of "meta-an-
        alysis," the author reviews five "classes
        of methods/data" in science studies for the
        purpose of illuminating "the criteria by
        which those studies claim to represent so-
        cial knowledge of scientific reality."

G65. Collins, H.M.

1981   "The Place of the 'Core-set' in Modern Sci-
        ence: Social Contingency with Methodologi-
        cal Propriety in Science." History of
        Science 19: 6-19.
        "For most scientific observational claims,
        at least in the case of modern science with
        its developed division of labor, there will
        be only a few scientists in a position to
        conduct tests. Only these few truly bear

the responsibility for methodological pro-
priety. . . . It is only by studying these
small sets of scientists ['core-sets']
that the methods of science can be properly
understood. . . ." Drawing on the controversies presented in Collins [G66], the
author argues that not only what are taken
to be "the constraints of theory . . . but
also the influence of fashion, 'world view,'
what I have called social contingency, will
affect the outcome of the debate over what
counts as a competent experiment, and hence
the outcome of scientific controversy."
At first glance, this is the power and rhetoric of elitism turned on its ear. For
more see Collins and Pinch [S49].

G66.   Collins, H.M. (ed.).

1981   "Special Issue on 'Knowledge and Controversy: Studies of Modern Natural Science."
Social Studies of Science 11 (February)

While I applaud the "empirical programme
of relativism," the editor's assurance that
"this collection . . .will obviate the
necessity for further defences and re-af-
firmation" gives me great pause. The case
studies by Travis, Collins, Pickering, Harvey, and Pinch are carefully constructed,
but the editor's need to draw programmatic
boundaries and cite literature parochially
ensures that "further defences" will be
necessary, expecially to non-Bath/non-Edin-
burgh Europeans and North American researchers of scientific controversy.

G67.   Geison, Gerald L.

1981   "Scientific Change, Emerging Specialties,
and Research Schools." History of Science
19: 20-40.
"During the past decade, several historians

and sociologists of science have begun to
focus attention on small groups of interacting scientists. The resulting literature, while thus far modest in its size
and achievements, suggests some intriguing
differences . . . [of grappling with] the
interaction between social and conceptual
factors in the scientific enterprise. . . .
[S]ociologists tend to focus on 'emerging
specialties,' while the historians tend
to focus on 'research schools'." Advocacy
of the latter plus a critique of Mulkay's
"branching model" [G22*] as deployed in
Astronomy Transformed [Edge and Mulkay,
P19] follows. The author underestimates
the size of the specialty literature and
contributes precious little new here to
its achievements.

CITATION-BASED: A Reference or Citation Approach to Specialty Definition and/or Analysis

C01. Garvey, W.D. and K. Tomita

1972 "Continuity of Productivity by Scientists in the Years 1968-71." Science Studies 2: 379-383.
A substantial minority of authors in nine disciplines changed research interest--and published accordingly--during the priod considered, a practice "so widespread . . . that it most probably is essential to scientific progress."

Griffith, B.C. and N.C. Mullins

1972 See [G02].

Krantz, D.L.

1972 See [S03].

Baker, A.R.H.

1973 See [S09].

C02. Small, Henry G.

1973 "Co-citation in the Scientific Literature: A New Measure of the Relationship between Two Documents." Journal of the American Society for Information Science 24: 265-269.
The paper that introduced the co-citation technique.

Spreitzer, E. and L.T. Reynolds

1973 See [S18].

C03. Cawkell, A.E.

1974 "Search Strategy, Construction and Use of Citation Networks, with a

Socio-scientific Example: "Amorphous
Semi-conductors and S.R. Ovshinsky."
Journal of the American Society for
Information Science 25 (March-April):
123-130.
See Gibbons and King [P02] for a com-
parison.

Duncan, S.S.

1974 See [S21].

Gilbert, G.N. and S. Woolgar

1974 See [G11].

C04. Griffith, B.C., H.G. Small, J.A. Stonehill,
and S. Dey

1974 "The Structure of Scientific Literature II: Toward a Macro and Micro-
structure for Science." Science Studies 4:339-365.
A continuation of the program introduced in Small [C02], Small and Griffith [G14].

C05. Magyar, George

1974 "Bibliometric Analysis of a New Research Sub-field." Journal of Documentation 30:32-40.
A statistical analysis of publications
in a physics subfield, "dye lasers,"
1966-72.

C06. Small, H.G.

1974 "Multiple Citation Patterns in Scientific Literature: The Circle and Hill
Models." Information Storage and Retrieval 10: 393-402.

"The concept of tri-citation is introduced, as a logical extension of
co-citation, and a geometrical model
(the circle model) is devised to account for these and all other forms
of multiple citation. . . . A further
refinement of the model is suggested
(the hill model) . . . Implications
of such spatial models for the representation of clusters of highly cited
documents are discussed [with an example from particle physics]."

Small, H. and B.C. Griffith

1974 See [G14].

C07   Wolek, Francis W. and Belver C. Griffith

1974 "Policy and Informal Communications
in Applied Science and Technology."
Science Studies 4: 411-420.
"Abstracting services, computerized
retrieval systems, review publications,
and decreased lead times have been,
and are, productive. However, the
ethic of efficiency is not adequate
as the sole guideline for policy on
communication and is especially limited for policy on the informal communications which are so central to
work in applied fields."

Cole, Stephen

1975 See [S28].

C08. Finison, L.J. and C.L. Whittemore

1975 "Linguistic Isolation of American
Social Psychology--A Comparative
Study of Journal Citations." American

Psychologist 30: 513-516.
The authors find a non-symmetric "imperialism of ideas": non-American social science is permeable to "American" ideas, but not vice versa.

C09. Stigler, G.J. and C. Friedland

1975 "The Citation Practices of Doctorates in Economics." _Journal of Political Economy_ 83: 477-507.
"In order to test the existence of 'schools of thought' . . . the authors tabulate the citation practices of the 1950-1955 economics doctorates from six major universities . . . in the fields of value theory and monetary theory" [I].

Breiger, R.L.

1976 See [B15].

C10. Narin, Francis

1976 _Evaluative Bibliometrics: The Use of Citation Analysis in the Evaluation of Scientific Activity._ New Jersey: Computer Horizons, Inc.
"Reviews the development of publication and citation counting techniques, and examines studies correlating literature based measures with other measures of quality and quantity of scientific output. Focuses on 'influence methodology,' a procedure for calculating the influence of individual journals. This technique facilitates the use of citation analysis to determine characteristics of aggregates of papers (representing departments, disciplines, schools, journals,

nations, etc.). 'Influence maps' describe patterns of influence for journals in biology, chemistry, physics, engineering, psychology, mathematics, earth and space sciences" [P].

C11. Price, D. de S. and S. Gursey

1976 "Studies in Scientometrics. Part I. Transience and Continuance in Scientific Authorship." International Forum on Information and Documentation 1: 17-24.
Establishes two opposite phenomena-- "transience and continuance in scientific authorship."

Studer, K.E. and D.E. Chubin

1976 See [B20].

C12. Winstanley, Monica

1976 "Assimilation into the Literature of a Critical Advance in Molecular Biology." Social Studies of Science 6: 545-549.
The author uses "citation analysis from a survey of books to study the rate of diffusion into formal education and into the popular literature, of the discovery of the double helical structure of the genetic material, DNA." The results demonstrate the slow diffusion of a new advance, even as profound as the double helix.

C13. Citation Studies of Scientific Specialties

1977 Special Issue. Social Studies of Science 7 (May).
Contains important papers by Small [B29], Sullivan et al. [G42, P28],

and Porter [C16].

Cole, S., J.R. Cole, and L. Dietrich

1977   See [G33].

C14.   Garfield, Eugene

1977   Essays of an Information Scientist,
        Volume 1 1962-1973; Volume 2, 1974-
        1976. Philadelphia: ISI Press.
        The "best of Garfield" in this two-
        volume collection of editorials pub-
        lished in Current Contents. The vi-
        sions of a pioneer in the creative
        management and analysis of literature
        materialize before our eyes.

C15.   Garfield, Eugene, Morton V. Malin, and
        Henry Small

1977   "Citation Data as Science Indica-
        tors." PP. 179-207 in Y. Elkana et
        al. (eds.), Toward a Metric of Sci-
        ence. New York: Wiley.
        "Section on social and cognitive
        structures of science discusses ex-
        periments using co-citation analysis
        to derive clusters of inter-related
        literature. . . . Maps of clusters
        of co-citations can demonstrate cur-
        rent linkages between disciplines;
        shifts in clusters over time may be
        used to investigate the nature of
        change in specialties" [P].

Gilbert, G. Nigel

1977   See [G36].

Griffith, B.C. M.C. Drott, and H.G. Small

1977   See [G37].

Mullins, N.C., L.L. Hargens, P.K. Hecht,
and E.L. Kick

1977   See [B25].

C16.   Porter, Alan L.

1977   "Citation Analysis: Queries and Ca-
        veats." Social Studies of Science
        7:257-267.
        This paper raises some sticky con-
        ceptual and methodological issues in
        citation analysis. "For instance,
        if close colleagues selectively each
        other's work for reasons other than
        scientific influence, will not re-
        sults be biased against the Ortega
        hypothesis?"

Small, H.G.

1977   See [B29].

C17.   Spiegel-Roesing, Ina

1977   "Science Studies: Bibliometric and
        Content Analysis." Social Studies
        of Science 7 (February): 97-113.

        An evaluation of all articles (n=66)
        published in the first four volumes
        (1971-1974) of this international,
        multidisciplinary journal. The cate-
        gory "development of disciplines and
        research areas" is found to represent
        20 (30.3%) of the articles published
        in the formative years of this now-
        prominent journal. Other dimensions

used to characterize this literature
include methodological approach, citation patterns and relevance.

C18. Studer, K.E.

1977   "Interpreting Scientific Growth: A
Comment on Derek Price's 'Science
Since Babylon.'" History of Science
15: 44-51.

Sullivan, D., D.H. White, and E.J. Barboni

1977   See [G42].

C19. Tagliacozzo, Renata

1977   "Self-Citations in Scientific Literature." Journal of Documentation 33
(December): 251-265.
Drawing on bibliographies of articles
in plant physiology and neurobiology,
the author finds "self-citations to
be more recent and to be cited more
frequently in the text of the citing
articles than citations of other authors. The extent of self-citing
did not appear to be related to the
number of co-authors and to the bibliography size of the citing articles, or to their authors' productivity." For self-citation findings
that differ in large part from these,
see Studer and Chubin [B52].

C20. Bavelas, Janet Beavin

1978   "The Social Psychology of Citations."
Canadian Psychological Review 19:
158-163.

C21. Ellis, P., G. Hepburn, and C. Oppenheim

1978 "Studies on Patent Citation Networks." Journal of Documentation
34: 12-20.
A "novel technique for displaying
the history of technological subjects
and their key turning points" is
described.

Small, H.G.

1978 See [G46].

Chubin, D.E. and K.E. Studer

1979 See [B38].

Edge, D.O.

1979 See [G51].

C22. Jones, Warren T. and Lucio Chiaraviglio

1979 "Is Science an Adaptive System?"
Behavioral Science 24: 325-333.

This article sustains "the hypothe-
sis that there are properties of
published scientific monographs
which, relative to the citing relations, are found to replicate and
recombine in a fashion that is formally identical to the replication
and recombination of genetic markers
of many viral systems." Seven subject categories were derived from
the Searchable Physics Information
(SPIN) hierarchical classification
system.

C23.   Krauze, T.R. and R. McGinnis

        1979   "A Matrix Analysis of Scientific
                Specialties and Careers in Science."
                Scientometrics 1 (August): 419:444.

                "Introduces the concept of 'scienti-
                fic space,' which provides a mathe-
                matical structure for exploring con-
                nections among scientific articles
                and their authors. . . . The authors
                suggest, 'within our approach to
                scientific space we should be able
                to reconstruct . . . not only the
                location of specialties within the
                wider disciplinary area but also
                their emergence, development and de-
                cline'" [P].

        Lenoir, Timothy

        1979   See [B45].

C24.   Moravcsik, M.S. and P. Murugesan

        1979   "Citation Patterns in Scientific
                Revolutions." Scientometrics 1
                (January): 161-169.
                A content analysis of citations in-
                volving two discoveries in physics:
                BCS theory of superconductivity and
                the non-conservation of parity.

        Small, H.G. and D. Crane

        1979   See [S61].

C25.   Vlachy, Jan

        1979   "Publication Output in Physics Sub-
                fields." Czechoslovakian Journal
                of Physics 29: 829-836.
                Figures and tables based on Physics

Abstracts categories of 1977-79
publications are cross-tabulated by
country.

C26. Vlachy, Jan

1979   "Mobility in Science: A Bibliography
        of Scientific Career Migration,
        Field Mobility, and International
        Academic Circulation and Brain
        Drain." Scientometrics 1: 201-228.
        For the years 1945-1978, 624 entries
        are presented in alphabetical order
        of author's surname.

White, D.H., D. Sullivan, and E.T. Barboni

1979   See [P40].

Hargens, Lowell L., Nicholas C. Mullins,
and Pamela K. Hecht

1980   See [B50].

C27. Lawson, Julia, Barbara Kostrewski, and
      C. Oppenheim

1980   "A Bibliometric Study of a New Sub-
        ject Field: Energy Analysis." Sci-
        entometrics 2: 227-237.
        "Examination of the titles of arti-
        cles [found in ISI sources] demon-
        strated that even after ten years
        there is no standard terminology in
        the area [of energy analysis]. This
        casts doubt on the value of search-
        ing by title terms for new inter-
        disciplinary subjects."

Morman, Edward T.

1980   See [G60].

Nadel, Edward

1980   See [P49].

C28.   Small, Henry

1980   "Co-citation Context Analysis and
        the Structure of Paradigms." Jour-
        nal of Documentation 36 (September):
        183-196.
        "The end product of the context
        analysis would be a network whose
        nodes, lines and regions are labelled
        according to the consensual usuage
        of the documents. How this struc-
        ture would compare with a more tra-
        ditional account of the state of a
        specialty written by a specialist
        remains to be seen, but the signifi-
        cance of this procedure is that for
        the first time we can arrive at a
        representation of consensual know-
        ledge--a paradigm--without the aid
        of an expert. . . . Finally for
        bibliometric studies, it would be
        possible to treat the literature of
        a subject as more that a 'black box'
        about which only rudimentary statis-
        tical facts can be ascertained.
        Bibliometrics could truly become a
        branch of epistemology." Lofty
        goals?

C29.   Small, H. and E. Greenlee

1980   "Citation Context Analysis of a
        Co-citation Cluster: Recombinant-
        DNA." Scientometrics 2 (July): 277-
        301.
        "The techniques of co-citation clus-
        tering and citation context analy-
        sis are combined to concretely

define the shared knowledge within
a research specialty."

Studer, K.E. and D.E. Chubin

1980   See [B52].

C30. Sullivan, D., D. Koester, D.H. White, and
      R. Kern

      1980   "Understanding Rapid Theoretical
              Change in Particle Phusics: A Month-
              by-Month Co-citation Analysis."
              Scientometrics 2: 309-319.
              The authors "present month-by-month
              co-citation analyses of key phases
              in the weak-electromagnetic unifica-
              tion research program within parti-
              cle physics and show that these ana-
              lyses capture and illuminate very
              rapid intellectual changes. . . .
              [Y]et another illustration of the
              utility of co-citation analysis for
              understanding the history of science"
              (see, for example, Sullivan et al.
              [P28]).

C31. White, Howard. and Belver C. Griffith

      1980   "Author Co-citation: A Literature
              Measure of Intellectual Structure."
              Unpublished paper.
              "[T]he mapping of a particular area
              of science, in this case information
              science, can be done using authors
              as units of analysis, and the co-ci-
              tations of pairs of authors as the
              variable that indicates their 'dis-
              tances' from each other. The analy-
              sis assumes that the more two authors
              are cited together, the closer the
              relationship between them. . . .
              The resulting map shows: identifiable

author groups (akin to 'schools')
of information science, . . . [as
well as] the degree of centrality
and peripherality of authors within
groups [and] proximities of authors
within groups and across group boundaries. . . . The technique establishes authors, as well as documents,
as an effective unit in analysing
subject specialties."

C32. Coward, H. Roberts and Henry Small

1981 "Tracking Scientific Specialty Development in the 1970s with Co-citation Clusters." Presented at Annual
Meeting, AAAS, Toronto (January).

"Graphic displays of specialty development in plate tectonics, pain
and neurotransmitter research, radio
astronomy, hypothalamic releasing-
hormones, and other areas [are] presented. Implications for a life-
cycle model of scientific specialties [are] discussed, including con-
siderations such as brancing or merg-
ing lines of research, specialty
life-time, and the rate of change
of knowledge."

C33. Cozzens, Susan E.

1981 "Taking the Measure of Science: A
Review of Citation Theories." International Society for the Sociology of Knowledge Newsletter 7
(May): 16-21.
The author presents overviews of
three orientations to citation data:
"the normative interpretation," "the
interpretive account," and "the symbolic perspective." Along the way,

she observes that "there is a reify-
ing tendency among citation analysts.
They tend to view their measures as
direct manifestations of certain
social constructs, without visuali-
zing at the same time the scientists
who create the citation patterns.
More attention to the theory of citing will bring those scientists
back into the sociological conscious-
ness." Amidst such observations and
exhortations, I detect a true be-
liever in citation analysis.

C34. Cronin, Blaise

1981   "The Need for a Theory of Citing."
         Journal of Documentation 37 (March):
         16-24.
         "Metaphorically speaking, citations
         are frozen footprints in the land-
         scape of scholarly achievement;
         footprints which bear witness to
         the passing of ideas." With such
         a prosaic beginning, the author re-
         views the multidisciplinary commen-
         tary on citation analysis and inter-
         pretation--in search of a "forensic
         tool."

C35. Griffith, Belver C.

1981   "Bibliographic Measures as Science
         Indicators." 4S Newsletter 6
         (Spring): 15-18.
         "Several broad problem areas have
         been examined by researchers study-
         ing scientific literatures and have
         generated research with potential
         policy implications. . . . [W]e .
         . . have used a variety of ways to
         subdivide science and study its

structure. However, only citation
methods, of all these, identifies
and focuses upon the research problem. There, I believe, is bibliographic measures' unique contribution to policy research . . . "

C36. Vlachy, Jan

1981   "Mobility in Physics: A Bibliography
of Occupational, Geographic and
Field Mobility of Physicists."
Czechoslovakian Journal of Physics
31: 669-674.
One hundred forty entries are presented for the years 1936-78.

PHYSICAL SCIENCE: Physics, Astronomy, Chemistry, Geology and Mathematics Specialties

P01. Gaston, Jerry

1972   "Communication and the Reward System of Science: A Study of a National 'Invisible College.'" Pp. 25-
41 in P. Halmos (ed.), The Sociology
of Science. The Sociological Review
Monograph 18 (September).

P02. Gibbons, Michael and Philip King

1972   "The Development of Ovonic Switches--
A Case Study of a Scientific Controversy." Science Studies 2: 295-
309.
Ovshinsky as a latter-day Velikovsky
in collision with the solid-state
physics community.

McGinnis, R. and V.P. Singh

1972   See [G04].

Morrell, J.B.

1972   See [L02].

Yellin, Joel

1972   See [G08].

P03. Zaltman, G. and B.M. Kohler

1972   "The Dissemination of Task and So-
ciomemotional Information in an International Community of Scientists."
Journal of the American Society for
Information Science 23: 225-236.
Based on a study sample of 977 theoretical high energy physicists

working in 35 countries, the authors
conclude that "information flowed
relatively freely accross geopoliti-
cal boundaries." Twenty-five (sub)
specialties are also examined for
diffusion of innovations--in number
and time--across national boundaries.

P04. Gaston, Jerry

1973   Originality and Competition in Science: A Study of the British High
Energy Physics Community. Chicago
and London: University of Chicago
Press.
"A study of the incidence and consequences of competition for priori-
ty among both theorists and experi-
mentalists in high energy physics"
[M]. With an emphasis on normative
behavior, the author's fasination
with social structure overshadows
questions of content--he is dis-
armed.

P04a. Woolgar, S.W.

1975   (Review). Philosophy of the Social
Sciences 5: 358-360.
"No study of informal communication
networks is complete without a discussion of the infamous 'invisible
college.' Accordingly, Gaston identifies a cluster of individuals .
. ." who might be both arbitrarily
defined and relatively isolated.

P05. Gillmor, C.S. and C.J. Terman

1973   "Communication Modes of Geophysics:

The Case of Ionospheric Physics."
EOS 54: 900-908.
"Discusses the growth of the field
of ionospheric physics [since 1920],
with particular attention given to
communication patterns and journal
specialization. . . . Several modes
of communication are examined: journals; personal informal meetings;
society meetings and conferences;
seminars; monographs; correspon-
dence. Different aspects of re-
search--technical information, current awareness, theory--are served
by different modes of communication.
Journals receive the highest rating
for serving all three aspects of
research. Society meetings are the
most effective mode for maintaining
current awareness, and monographs
are the best mode of theory dissemination" [P].

P06. Law, John

1973   "The Development of Specialties
        in Science: The Case of X-Ray Pro-
        tein Crystallography." Science
        Studies 3: 275-303.
        Hypothesizes three types of spe-
        cialties: technique- or method-based,
        theory-based, and subject matter-
        based. Such a well-delineated ty-
        pology may fit certain sciences
        but not others; in its elegance the
        typology is premature.

P07. Mulkay, M.J. and D.O. Edge

1973   "Cognitive, Technical and Social
        Factors in the Growth of Radio
        Astronomy." Social Science Infor-

mation 12 (December): 25-61.
An early report treated fully in
Edge and Mulkay [P19].

P08. Collins, H.M.

1974   "The TEA Set: Tacit Knowledge and
        Scientific Networks." Science
        Studies 4: 165-186.
        "[A]ll types of knowledge involve
        tacit rules which are impossible
        to formulate explicitly in full.
        The diffusion of such tacit know-
        ledge is examined in relation to
        one research network concerned
        with building TEA lasers " [M].

P09. Holton, Gerald

1974   "Striking Gold in Science: Fermi's
        Group and the Recapture of Italy's
        Place in Physics." Minerva 12
        (April): 159-198.
        Fermi's group, modeled on a family,
        helped physics "come of age" in the
        1930s, "in terms of support--finan-
        cial and institutional--recruit-
        ment, opportunities for careers and
        national and international recog-
        nition."

P10. Holloway, David

1974   "Innovation in Science--The Case
        of Cybernetics in the Soviet Union."
        Science Studies 4: 299-337.
        "A study of the interplay of inter-
        nal and external factors in the
        development of cybernetics in Rus-
        sia" [M].

P11. Mitroff, Ian I.

  1974   The Subjective Side of Science:
         A Philosophical Inquiry into the
         the Psychology of the Apollo Moon
         Scientists. New York: Elsevier.

         A collective biography of moon sci-
         entists' epistemologies and intel-
         lectual commitments--as revealed
         through public and private state-
         ments.

P12. Mitroff, I.I. and R.O. Mason

  1974   "On Evaluating the Scientific Con-
         tribution of the Apollo Moon Mis-
         sions via Information Theory: A
         Study of the Scientist-Scientist Re-
         lationship." Management Science
         20 (August): 1501-1513.

      Mulkay, M.J.

  1974   See [G12].

P13. Zaltman, Gerald

  1974   "A Note on International Invisible
         College for Information Exchange."
         Journal of the American Society for
         Information Science 25: 113-117.

         Various measures of communication
         are presented to establish the exis-
         tence of a theoretical high-energy
         physics network of researchers.

P14. Collins, H.M.

  1974   "The Seven Sexes: A Study in the
         Sociology of a Phenomenon, or the
         Replication of Experiments in Physics."

112

Sociology 9: 205-224.
This study of research on gravita-
tional waves asks, "What is a replication?". The answer derives
from scientific beliefs which themselves are socially contingent.

Collins, H.M. and R.G. Harrison

1975   See [L06].

P15. Hargens, Lowell L.

1975   Patterns of Scientific Research:
        A Comparative Analysis of Research
        in Three Scientific Fields. Wash-
        ington, DC: American Sociological
        Association.

P15a. Chubin, Daryl E.

1976   (Review). Contemporary Sociology
        5 (September): 685-687.
        Hargens compares a sample of Ph.D.
        scientists in chemistry, mathema-
        tics, and political science employed
        by American universities. He "pos-
        tualtes that the three fields can
        be differentiated on three dimen-
        sions: specialization, normative
        integration, and functional inte-
        gration." While specialization is
        never invoked as an explanatory
        variable, what is here "is techni-
        cally sound, provocative, and has
        been superseded . . . ."

P16. Barboni, E.J.

1976   Functional Diffentiation and Tech-
        nological Specialization in a Spe-
        cialty in High Energy Physics:

The Case of Weak Interactions of
Elementary Particles. Cornell
University: Unpublished Ph.D. dis-
sertation.

P17. Blau, Judith R.

1976   "Scientific Recognition: Academic
Context and Professional Role."
Social Studies of Science 6: 533-
545.
A Merton-inspired study of the A-
merican theoretical high energy
physics community that draws on
the author's unpublished Ph.D. dissertation (The Structure of Science,
Northwestern University, 1972).

P18. Dolby, R.G.A.

1976   "The Case of Physical Chemistry."
Pp. 63-73 in G. Lemaine et al.
(eds.), [G25].
"Traces the development of physical chemistry, in order to examine
the relative role of social and
cognitive factors in the emergence
of a new discipline. Compares national differences (Germany, France,
Britain, America) in institutions
and in internal developments in
chemistry, and examines how the
differences affect the development
of physical chemistry at four stages: (1) the appearance of new
ideas and techniques at the periphery of the established fields;
(2) the formation of localized
groups that explore and expand the
idea, and train students; (3) the
diffusion of the group, with their
distinctive interests and skills

maintained; (4) the achievement of institutional status as a separate discipline" [P].

P19.   Edge, D.O. and M.J. Mulkay

1976   Astronomy Transformed: The Emergence of Radio Astronomy in Britain. New York: Wiley.
"Judgements of scientific importance tend to be made in relation to a group's technical equipment. Yet technical development itself depends on the group's research strategy, which, in turn, is conditioned by perceptions of scientific significance. As a result of the interdependence between these factors the research groups at Cambridge and Jodrell Bank, having entered radio astronomy from different directions, have continued [into the 1970s] to develop along distinct lines in their use of techniques, in their areas of interest and in their overall strategies." The authors go on to compare their case study with the findings of six selected others, including Mullins on the phage group, Ben-David and Collins on psychology, and Fisher on Invariant Theorists, and call for comparative (cross-field) studies that pay "much more attention to the science (i.e., the 'culture')" than has been customary.

P19a. Crane, Diana

1977   (Review). Newsletter of the Society for Social Studies of Science 2 (Fall): 27-29.

"The richness of detail which [the
authors] present to the reader is
both an asset and a liability. On
the one hand, this mass of information gives the reader the sense
of truly participating in the development of a specialty . . .
On the other hand, their unwilling-
ness to apply any theoretical
framework to their historical account . . . makes their book difficult to read and less useful than
it might have been . . . A specialty which relied on such expen-
sive instrumentation must have had
complex interrelationships with
science policy-making committees.
How decisions at the governmental
level affected the development of
the field is only touched upon
briefly."

P19b. Sullivan, D.F. and D.H. White

1977   (Review). Newsletter of the Socie-
        ty for Social Studies of Science
        2 (Fall): 25-27.
        "[The book] offers the first de-
        tailed study of the social and
        intellectual properties of a sci-
        entific specialty involving high
        technology. . . . [A]s we better
        understand the cases we have and
        analyze more cases of scientific
        specialty growth and development,
        there are a few commonalities (e.
        g., the role of marginals in spe-
        cialty formation) but many diver-
        gencies. This result precludes
        an optimistic view that the pro-
        blems faced by the sociology of
        science are simple . . ."

P19c. Gieryn, Thomas F.

1977 (Review). <u>Contemporary Sociology</u> 6
      (November): 656-658.
      "[The authors'] choice of a pointil-
      list portrait of the history of radio
      astronomy results from a theoretical
      commitment to a certain explanation
      of scientific change, and not from
      theoretical agnosticism. . . . <u>Astro-
      nomy Transformed</u> has raised the ante
      for future sociological studies of
      specialty formation in science. In
      its sensitive attention to the details
      of cognitive structures . . . the work
      is a masterpiece of the historical
      sociology of scientific knowledge."

P19d. Chubin, Daryl E.

1978 (Review). <u>Technology and Culture</u> 19
      (July): 580-583.
      "The authors conducted twenty exten-
      sive interviews with the innovators
      of radar, radio, and optical astro-
      nomy and fulfilled, in full measure,
      their two aims: first, 'that of pro-
      viding a case study showing how the
      social and intellectual aspects of
      radio astronomy have been linked to-
      gether in one historical process,'
      and second, to 'discuss the findings
      of this case study in relation to
      previous writings on the development
      of areas of scientific inquiry.' That
      nine chapters (85 percent of the text)
      are consumed by the first aim, leaving
      one chapter for 'some sociological
      implications,' may seem an undue im-
      balance. . . . If the reader feels
      engulfed by detail while plodding
      through the copious anectdotal ex-
      cerpts, it is because the authors

chose to interrupt the flow of the
narrative to convey how the science
got done. . . . As for the remaining
sociological analysis, I am puzzled
as to why (1) Crane's work, which pre-
dated Mullins's, is barely alluded to,
while Kuhn and Hagstrom are treated
at length. (2) In the discussion of
teams and the importance of students--
which is underplayed for my taste--
Zuckerman's research on Nobel laureates
is not cited. The element of social
heritability in receiving the prize
may well extend beyond elite scientists.
This could have been explored in the
present case, particularly within the
discussion of 'intellectual migration'
and the origins of innovations. (3)
External constraints, not just the
availability of research funds and
Britain's centralized funding policy,
but broader cultural themes to which
European science analysts are so sen-
sitive, were seldom in evidence." Re-
gardless, the book remains a touchstone
for future studies of scientific specialties.

P20. Frankel, Eugene

1976 "Corpuscular Optics and the Wave Theory
of Light: The Science and Politics of
a Revolution in Physics." Social Studies of Science 6: 141-184.
"We find that a state of crisis need
not characterize a field as a whole
prior to a scientific revolution. . . .
[S]ocial and political factors, which
Kuhn rightly regards as crucial for
the resolution of scientific revolutions, seem equally important for the
initiation of revolutions as well."

P21. Gilbert, G. Nigel

1976 "The Transformation of Research Findings into Scientific Knowledge." Social Studies of Science 6: 281-306.

A study of the "context of justification" in which "only the procedures actually used by natural scientists to decide on the validity of claims to scientific knowledge" are considered. Further development of this study, based on the problem area known as "radar meteor research" is contained in Gilbert [P22].

P22. Gilbert, G. Nigel

1976 "The Development of Science and Scientific Knowledge: The Case of Radar Meteor Research." Pp. 187-204 in G. Lemaine et al. [G25].

P23. O'Connor, Jean G. and Arthur J. Meadows

1976 "Specialization and Professionalization in British Geology." Social Studies of Science 6: 77-89.
"Rather little detailed study has yet been carried out into the process of professional-amateur differentiation within specific scientific disciplines. The present paper examines one particularly important aspect of this differentiation in British geology--its relationship to specialization in research and to communication activities (especially via membership of geological societies)."

Robbins, David and Ron Johnston

1976 See [G27].

Woolgar, S.W.

1976   See [G31].

P24.   Wynne, Brian

1976   "C.G. Barkla and the J Phenomenon."
Social Studies of Science 6: 307-347.

A case study of cognitive deviance in
physics and how rationality is socially
negotiated and redefined to accommo-
date the power of an eminent physicist.

P25.   Edge, D.O.

1977   "The Sociology of Innovation in Modern
Astronomy." Quarterly Journal of the
Royal Astronomical Society 18: 326-
339.

P26.   Moseley, Russell

1977   "Tadpoles and Frogs: Some Aspects of
the Professionalization of British
Physics, 1870-1939." Social Studies
of Science 7: 423-446.
"Granting the importance of educational
factors and the growth of specialization for scientific professionalization in general, there appears to be
a case for . . . the locus of power
within the scientific community, and
of the tensions between the elite and
rank and file. Any comprehensive study of the social organization of science in Britain will have to recognize
that the tadpoles can be as interesting and as important, as the frogs."

P27.   Pinch, Trevor

1977   "What Does a Proof Do if It Does Not

Prove?" Pp. 171-215 in E. Mendelsohn et al. (eds.), The Social Production of Scientific Knowledge. Sociology of the Sciences, Vol. 1. Dordrecht and Boston: D. Reidel. An intriguing account of communication failure in quantrum physics.

Pyenson, Lewis and Douglas Skopp

1977 See [G41].

P28. Sullivan, D., D.H. White, and E.J. Barboni

1977 "The State of a Science: Indicators in the Specialty of Weak Interactions." Social Studies of Science 7 (May): 167-200. The first in a series of papers on the evolution of post-World War II research on weak interactions of elementary particles. The attempt to combine intellectual history with quantitative analysis of author productivity and citation patterns is laudable--and illustrative of the fruitful collaboration between an "insider" (DHW, experimental physicist) and an "outsider" (DS, sociologist of science) [see, e.g., P41].

Sullivan, D., D.H. White, and E.J. Barboni

1977 See [G42].

P29. Blau, Judith R.

1978 "Sociometric Structure of a Scientific Discipline." Research in Sociology of Knowledge, Sciences and Art 1: 191-206. A sociometric analysis of 411 U.S.

theoretical high-energy physicists yields: "(a) an invisible college of 111 physicists comprising a single network, (b) a periphery of 125 physicists who are members of separate clusters consisting of 2-18 members, and (c) 175 isolates who do not consult any colleagues outside their own institution' . . . by eliminating the problematics in areas in which they are best qualified."

P30. Brush, Stephen

1978 "Planetary Science: From Underground to Underdog." Scientia 113 (Autumn): 771-787.
"Examines the effect of a hierarchy among subfields of physics on the definition of fundamental issues, on career choice, and on historical interpretation. . . ." Change in the status of planetary physics "is traced not only to the effects of specialization and professionalization, but to the role of particular scientists and events" [P].

Friedkin, N.E.

1978 See [G43].

P31. Gaston, Jerry

1978 The Reward System in British and American Science. New York: Wiley.

A defense of Mertonian sociology of marginal interest to the student of specialties (see reviews by Ziman [P31a] and Woolgar [P31b]).

P31a. Ziman, John

       1979 (Review). American Journal of Socio-
             logy 85 (November): 676-678.

P31b. Woolgar, Steve

       1981 (Review). Isis 72: 297-298.

       Gieryn, Thomas F.

       1978 See [G44].

P32.   Guntau, Martin

       1978 "The Emergence of Geology as a Scien-
             tific Discipline." History of Science
             16: 280-290.

             The author's point of departure are
             the widely differing opinions "as to
             the importance of different natural-
             ists for the development of geology
             as a discipline . . . [and] the cri-
             teria for historical evaluations in
             this subject."

P33.   Kevles, Daniel J.

       1978 The Physicists: The History of a Sci-
             entific Community in Modern America.
             New York: Random House.

P33a. Moyer, Albert E.

       1978 (Review). Isis 69: 634.
             "It is the first comprehensive history
             of the institutions, individuals, and
             scientific ideas of the modern Ameri-
             can physics community. . . . [it] is
             not purely an impersonal social or
             institutional history. Biographies

of individual scientists enliven nearly every chapter. . . . [According
to Kevles] . . . the physics community has been animated by a tension between traditional elitist leanings
and American democratic ideals."

P33b. Kargon, Robert

1978 "Physics in the United States" (Review). Science 204 (3 February): 524-
525.

"Kevles's story really begins in 1883
when Henry Rowland, a physicist at
Johns Hopkins and one of the America's
leading producers of physicists, appeared before the American Association
for the Advancement of cience . . ."
with a program of "best-science eliti-
cism." Kevles chronicles this eliti-
cism through two world wars, the Op-
penheimer case and McCarthyite incur-
sions of the 1950's, and the rise of
pork-barrel science in the 1960's.
"The real strength of the book lies
in its forthright presentation of the
public posture of the community."

P34. Kruytbosch, Carlos with Susan Papenfuss

1978 "Some Social and Organizational Cha-
racteristics of Breakthrough Science:
An Analysis of Major Innovations in
Four Fields of Science, 1950-1976."
Presented at Ninth World Congress of
Sociology, Uppsala, Sweden (August).

"Identifies 85 advances in the disciplines of astronomy, chemistry, earth
sciences and mathematics, and examines
the role of the National Science Foundation in funding research that lead
to the advances" [P]. An updated

124

"Project Hindsight"?

P35.   Hufbauer, Karl

1978   "The Role of Inter-specialty Migrants
        in Scientific Innovation: The Case of
        Research on the Stellar-energy Pro-
        blem, 1919-1938." Presented at the
        Third Annual Meeting of the Society
        for Social Studies of Science, Bloom-
        ington, Indiana (4-6 November).
        Introduces the status of temporary
        "interlopers" in addition to permanent
        "migrants."

P36.   Martin, B.R.

1978   "Radio Astronomy Revisited: A Reas-
        sessment of the Role of Competition
        and Conflict in the Development of
        Radio Astronomy." Sociological Review
        26 (February): 27-55.
        A reappraisal of Edge and Mulkay's
        [P19] analysis.

P37.   McCann, H. Gilman

1978   Chemistry Transformed: The Paradigma-
        tic Shift from Phlogiston to Oxygen.
        Norwood, N.J.: Ablex.
        This attempt to apply Kuhn's theory
        of scientific revolutions proceeds
        without the benefit of European scho-
        larship. The result is numerological
        and unabashed hypothesis-testing.

P37a.   Hufbauer, Karl

1979   "A Test of the Kuhnian Theory" (Re-
        view). Science 204 (18 May): 744-
        745.
        "In specifying the theory of scienti-
        fic revolutions, McCann makes two
        sorts of claims--some about the broad

developments that are likely to accom-
pany a scientific revolution and some
about the scientists who are likely
to be recruited to a revolutionary
paradigm. . . . While McCann mar-
shalls considerable evidence for his
trend hypotheses, he fails to make
an effective case for his propositions
regarding recruitment. The trouble
is that he takes articles, rather than
chemists, as the basic units of analysis. As a result, a few prolific re-
volutionaries dominate his statistics . . ."

P37b. Hargens, Lowell L.

1981 (Review). Contemporary Sociology 10
(March): 264-265.
". . . a quantitative analysis of
eighteenth-century chemists' abandon-
ment of the phlogiston theory in fa-
vor of Lavoisier's oxygen theory. . . .
McCann's historical account of the
theoretical transition also suggests
that the oxygen theory triumphed not
because the chemical community ex-
perienced what Kuhn labels a "crisis"
but because Lavoisier was able to convince strategic members of the community of the superiority of the oxygen
theory."

P38. Smith, Crosbie

1978 "A New Chart for British Natural Phi-
losophy: The Development of Energy
Physics in the Nineteenth Century."
History of Science 16: 231-279.

". . . simple internalist or externalist historiographical categories are
inadequate for an understanding of

the ways in which energy physics was important to nineteenth-century British physical scientists."

Barnes, Barry and Steven Shapin (eds.)

1979   See [G49].

Jordanova, Ludmilla J. and Ray S. Porter (eds.)

1979   See [B42].

P39.   Lankford, John

1979   "Amateur Versus Professional: The Transatlantic Debate over the Measurement of Jovian Longitude." Journal of the British Astronomy Association 89 (October): 574-582. "After 1880 professionalization played a key role in the transformation of astronomy. One major consequence involved was the re-definition of the status of amateurs. . . . [A]mateurs concentrated mainly on observation and description, but professionals had more complex goals. . . . This paper traces the antagonism, and its resolution when the American astronomers began to concentrate on the 'new astronomy' (astrophysics) leaving . . . planetary observations in the hands of amateurs."

P40.   White, D.H., D. Sullivan, and E.J. Barboni

1979   "The Interdependence of Theory and Experiment in Revolutionary Science: The Case of Parity Violation." Social Studies of Science 9 (August): 303-

327.

"An examination, primarily through citation analysis, is made of the changing interdependence of theory and experiment in a specialty within particle physics, the physics of weak interactions, during a period of rapid intellectual development. Lakatos' notions of how theory and experiment should be related during 'progressive' and 'stagnating' periods are used as guides for the analysis."

P41. White, D.H. and D. Sullivan

1979 "Social Currents in the Weak Interactions." Physics Today (April): 40-47.

P42. Wynne, Brian

1979 "Between Orthodoxy and Oblivion: The Normalisation of Deviance in Science." Pp. 67-84 in R. Wallis (ed.), [G56]. More on Barkla and the "J phenomenon."

P43. Crane, Diana

1980 "An Exploratory Study of Kuhnian Paradigms in Theoretical High Energy Physics." Social Studies of Science 10: 23-54. "An exploratory study of the characteristics of paradigms in theoretical high energy physics indicates that [among others] . . . the reception accorded a new theory by high energy theorists is a function of its breadth and testability . . . and the process of cognitive change in high energy theory did not, at least from 1960-75, follow the sequence of anomaly, crisis, and revolution." Credit is due

the author for attempting to apply
Kuhn's theory to explain "cognitive
change in a scientific specialty."

P44.* Pickering, Andy

 1980 "Exemplars and Analogies: A Comment
       on Crane's Study of Kuhnian Paradigms
       in High Energy Physics." Social Stu-
       dies of Science 10 (November): 497-
       502.
       "Crane is right to stress the impor-
       tance of Kuhn's concept of an exemplar
       for our understanding of the construc-
       tion of scientific knowledge. However,
       a more fundamental characterization
       of the nature of exemplars than she
       supplies is required, and her resort
       to evaluative standards as an explana-
       tory tool obscures more than it illu-
       minates. . . . Crane has investigated
       the working of only the theoretical
       HEP community, while the significance
       of testability surely derives from
       the complex interaction between theo-
       rists, phenomenologists and experimen-
       talists, and this is a matter which
       cannot be discussed without empirical
       investigation and analysis of the in-
       terpenetration of theoretical and ex-
       perimental practice."

P45.* Crane, Diana

 1980 "Reply to Pickering." Social Studies
       of Science 10: 502-506.
       ". . . there are more promising alter-
       natives than simply labeling innova-
       tions as analogies." These alterna-
       tives apparently do not reside where
       Pickering suggest they do. Verdict:
       This exchange typifies the gap that

exists between European and mainstream
North American approaches to science.
The arguments and evidence of each
lack compelling status for the other.
Yet as Pickering in his final (super-
fluous?) "Reply to Crane" (same issue,
507-508), observes: I can see no <u>ne-
cessary</u> incompatibility between our
two accounts . . ."

P46. Fleck, James

1980 "Development and Establishment Intelligence." Presented at Conference
on Scientific Establishments and Hierarchies, Oxford University (July).
The paper discusses the organizational
role of an elite, or scientific establishment, in the emergence of an "ar-
tificial intelligence" specialty in
the U.K. This detailed case study
is based on the author's M.Sc. thesis,
University of Manchester, and his Ph.D.
dissertation in progress there.

P47. Harvey, Bill

1980 "The Effects of Social Context on the
Process of Scientific Investigation:
Experimental Tests of Quantum Mecha-
nics." Pp. 139-163 in K.D. Knorr et
al. (eds.), [L15].

P48. Law, John

1980 "Fragmentation and Investment in Sedi-
mentology." <u>Social Studies of Science</u>
10 (February): 1-22.
"The decline of a formerly popular
method in sedimentology--that of particle size analysis . . . is explained
in terms of a simple model of scienti-

fic interest and investment in resources. . . . In a complex observational
science such as geology . . . actors
are well advised to 'invest' in a number of such techniques . . . This
makes for theoretical and methodological pluralism, and accounts for the
lack of acute crisis when one method
falls into disrepute."

P49.   Nadel, Edward

1980   "Multivariate Citation Analysis and
the Changing Cognitive Organization
in a Specialty of Physics." Social
Studies of Science 10: 449-473.
The author asks the useful question,
"[C]an we safely ignore historical
periods that lack major empirical,
methodological or theoretical events?
Are such periods intellectually sta-
tic backwaters, or do they contain a
high degree of intellectual activity?
In this paper we closely scrutinize
such periods in the development of a
particular specialty--superconducti-
vity in physics [1930-1956]--to see
whether the formal intellectual structure of the specialty was relatively
stagnant or changing in some way that
it would be important to understand."
Citation analysis and factor analysis
are selected and then combined as the
means to understanding.

P50.   Pickering, Andrew

1980   "The Role of Interests in High-Energy
Physics: The Choice between Charm and
Colour." Pp. 107-138 in K.D. Knorr
et al. (eds.), [L15].

131

P51. Pinch, T.J.

1980 "Theoreticians and the Production of
Experimental Anomaly: The Case of So-
lar Neutrinos." Pp. 77-106 in K.D.
Knorr et al. (eds.), [L15].

P52. Sullivan, D., E.J. Barboni, and D.H. White

1980 "Problem Choice and the Sociology of
Scientific Competition: An Interna-
tional Case Study in Particle Physics."
Knowledge and Society: Studies in the
Sociology of Culture Past and Present
3: 163-197.

P53. Weart, Spencer R.

1980 Scientists in Power. Cambridge, Mass.:
Harvard University Press.

P53a. Hughes, Phillip S.

1980 (Review). Contemporary Sociology 9
(September): 688-689.
" . . . at once a history of scientists, scientific ideas, scientific
institutions, and the politics of science, written with an exemplary use
of historical data. Weart relates
the political career of French nuclear
scientists over the first half of this
century . . ."

Collins, H.M. (ed.)

1981 See [G66].

P54. De Vorkin, David H.

1981 "Community and Spectral Classification in Astrophysics: The Acceptance
of E.C. Pickering's System in 1910."

132

Isis 72: 29-49.
"It took just over fifty years for
a consensus to appear on classification. During these fifty years astrophysics grew from being little more
than a novelty for many classical
nineteenth-century astronomers to what
was hailed as the 'New Astronomy'--
the revolutionary study of the physics
of the sun and stars. . . . More significant than the order of factors
favoring Pickering's system is that
a community of opinion was in force."

P55.   Gieryn, T.F.

1981   "The Aging of a Science and Its Ex-
ploitation of Innovation: Lessons from
X-Ray and Radio Astronomy." Scientometrics 3: 325-334.
"Analysis of the growth of radio and
X-ray astronomy in the 1960s suggests
that future reductions in the size
of entering cohorts of new doctorates
in astronomy may lengthen the time
needed to exploit future innovations,
discoveries or breakthroughs. This
may well lead to slower rates of advancement in astronomical knowledge."
This paper continues the author's work
as reported in Gieryn [G44].

P56.   Hall, D.H.

1981   "The Earth and Planetary Sciences
in Science During the Twentieth Century." Scientometrics 3: 349-362.

A bibliometric study based on coverage
in Science and Nature for the period
1900-1976.

P57. Kochen, M. and A. Blaivas

1981 "A Model for the Growth of Mathematical Specialties." Scientometrics 3: 265: 273.
"A mathematical model for the growth of two coupled mathematical specialties, differential geometry and topology, is analyzed. The key variable is the number of theorems in use in each specialty." Elegance overgeneralized.

P58. Nadel, Edward

1981 "Citation and Co-citation Indicators of a Phased Impact of the BCS Theory in the Physics of Superconductivity." Scientometrics 3 (May): 203-221.
More of the co-citation-factor analytic approach to the physics of superconductivty 1930-1964. Two of the last six historical periods (since 1957) are analyzed here [see Nadel, P49].

Traweek, Sharon

1981 See [L29].

P59. Vlachy, Jan

1981 "Mobility and Career Outlook for Physicists." Czechoslovak Journal of Physics 31: 675-686.
The paper includes a useful discussion of "mobility among physics subfields," data on U.S. physicists at all degree levels, and a 112-item bibliography.

P60. Vlachy, Jan

1981 "Physics in Europe: A Guide of Data Sources, Analyses and Documents." Czechoslovak Journal of Physics 31:

1-69.
"The almost 2000 entries on 30 countries . . . [are base on] a systematic
search through major journals, abstracting periodicals since the early
fifties, and scientometric collections
. . ." Of the four categories used,
"physics information, communication
patterns, social phenomena" accounts
for 12 percent of the entries, "science
disciplines including physics, organization and data" for 14.5 percent.

BIOMEDICAL SCIENCE: Biological, Biomedical, and Agricultural Specialties

B01.   Mullins, N.C.

1972   "The Development of a Scientific Specialty: The Phage group and the Origins of Molecular Biology." Minerva 10 (January): 52-82.
A classic case study which laid the groundwork for Mullins' subsequent modelling efforts [e.g., S15]. "Traces the transition of the Phage Group from shared interest to institutionalization. Examines social processes and intellectual problems for the following stages: paradigm group (1935-1945), communication network (1945-1953), cluster (1954-1962) and specialty (1962-1966). Cites conditions of luck, leadership, identification of a substantial problem, and institutional stability as factors in development" [P].

B02.   Kohler, R.E.

1973   "The Enzyme Theory and the Origin of Biochemistry." Isis 64: 181-196.

"The older historiography obviously has neglected the complex, uneven ways in which new ideas have become accepted as the basis for new disciplines. . . . I will argue that this new science [biochemistry] was associated with a new general theory of life processes, based on a new awareness of the importance on enzymes, and that this new view can be traced to several definite events which occurred in the 1890s."

136

B03. Rothschuh, K.E.

    1973 History of Physiology. Huntington, NY:
          Krieger.

B04. Schwartzbaum, Allan M., John H. McGrath,
    and Robert A. Rothman

    1973 "The Perception of Prestige Differences
          among Medical Subspecialties." Social
          Science and Medicine 7: 365-371.
          A professionalization-and-prestige ap-
          proach which reveals that physicians,
          in terms of organization and interac-
          tion, are anything but a homogeneous
          group.

B05. Maugh, Thomas H.

    1974 "Chemical Carcinogenesis: A Long-Ne-
          glected Field Blossoms." Science 183
          (8 March): 940-944.

B06. Olby, Robert

    1974 "The Origins of Molecular Genetics."
          Journal of the History of Biology 7
          (Spring): 93-100.

B07. Olby, Robert

    1974 The Path to the Double Helix. Seattle:
          University of Washington Press.

          Crick's version of the Crick-Watson
          priority race with Pauling and Wilkins
          and the enduring intellectual reper-
          cussions.

B07a. Teich, Mikulas

    1975 "A Single Path to the Double Helix?"
          (Review). Science 204 (18 May): 726-

727.
"Few subjects have attracted more attention in recent years than the Wat-
son-Crick model and as it belongs very
much to 'contemporary' history, the
historian's task to deal with it is
not made any easier." An interesting
lament.

B08. Rose, Hilary and Steven Rose

1974 "Do Not Adjust Your Mind, There Is a
Fault in Reality: Ideology in the Neu-
robiological Science." Pp. 148-171
in R.D. Whitley (ed.), Social Processes of Scientific Development. London:
Routledge and Kegan Paul.
Radical externalist sociology par ex-
cellence. The authors are among a
handful or so of Marxist scholars who
publish on science.

B09. Zuckerman, H.A.

1974 "The Emergence of a New Scientific
Paradigm: Bacterial Genetics as a Pro-
totypical Case." Presented at Annual
Meeting, American Sociological Association, Montreal.

B10. Backman, Carl B.

1975 "The Literature and Funding of Reproductive Physiology of Nonhuman Pri-
mates: A Preliminary Analysis." Cornell University: unpublished paper.

A time-series analysis utilizing NIH
and Index Medicus data.

B11. Bryant, Ian

1975 "Theories and Methods for a Sociolo-

138

gical History of Science: The Case of Victorian Physiology." Presented at the Conference on the Sociology of Science, University of York (September).

B12.   Farrall, Lyndsay A.

       1975   "Controversy and Conflict in Science: A Case Study--The English Biometric School and Mendel's Laws." Social Studies of Science 5: 269-301.
              "[T]he Mendelian-biometry dispute is examined first from the point of view that controversy and conflict in science can be the result of substantive differences about 'theory, methodology and research techniques.' This is followed by a discussion of the personal conflict and alienation between the scientists involved in the dispute."

B13.   Katz, Shaul and Joseph Ben-David

       1975   "Scientific Research and Agricultural Innovation in Israel." Minerva 13: 152-182.
              An historical study (1920-70) of the "academisation" of research and patterns of communication between scientists and agriculturists.

B14.   Markle, G.E. and J.W. Fox

       1975   "Paradigms or Public Relations: The Case of Social Biology." Presented at Annual Meeting, American Sociological Association, San Francisco (August).

B15.   Woolf, Patricia K.

       1975   "The Second Messenger: Informal Com-

munication in Cyclic AMP Research."
Minerva 14: 349-373.
A glimpse of the facilitating role
played by Gordon Conferences for biomedical researchers.

B16. Breiger, Ronald L.

1976 "Career Attributes and Network Structure: A Blockmodel Study of a Biomedical Research Specialty." American
Sociological Review 41 (February):
117-135.
Methodology runs amuck--beginning with
a co-citation cluster. For a critique, see Chubin et al. [G32].

B17. Fruton, J.S.

1976 "The Emergence of Biochemistry."
Science 192 (23 April): 327-334.

B18. Kohler, Robert E.

1976 "The Management of Science: The Experience of Warren Weaver and the
Rockefeller Foundation Programme in
Molecular Biology." Minerva 14 (Autumn): 279-306.
An exemplar of the social history of
science.

B19. Krohn, Wolfgang and Wolf Schafer

1976 "The Origins and Structure of Agricultural Chemistry." Pp. 22-27 in
G. Lemaine et al. [G25].
"Explores the influence of social
needs on the emergence and formation
of fundamental theories, and suggests
that agricultural chemistry is one of
the earliest examples of successful

140

goal-oriented theory development" [P].

B20.   Sadler, Judith

1976   "Elites in Science: A Study of Elites
in Relation to the Cognitive Structure
and Social Organization of Cancer Research." University of Manchester:
Unpublished M.Sc. thesis.
A study inspired by the work of Whitley [G16].

B21.   Studer, K.E. and D.E. Chubin

1976   "The Heroic Age of Reproductive Endo-
crinology: Its Development and Structure." Proceedings of the First Annual
Meeting, Society for Social Studies
of Science, Cornell University, Itha-
ca, NY (November).
Citation analysis versus participant-
scientists' retrospective accounts of
a specialty.

B22.   Tobey, Ronald

1976   "American Grassland Ecology, 1887-1955:
The Life Cycle of a Professional Re-
search Community." Presented at the
International Symposium on Quantitative
Methods in the History of Science, Ber-
keley (August).

B23.   Worboys, Michael

1976   "The Emergence of Tropical Medicine:
A Study in the Establishment of a Scientific Specialty." Pp. 75-98 in G.
Lemaine et al. [G25].
"Examines social and intellectual factors that influenced the emergence of
tropical medicine as a recognized field

of research,. teaching and professional
practice in the British Empire. Discusses the intellectual background
provided by 19th century biology and
. . . the political and economic imperialism of the period" [P].

Chubin, D.E., P.T. Carroll, and K.E. Studer

1977 See [G32].

B24. Egerton, Frank N.

1977 "A Bibliographical Guide to the History of General Ecology and Population
Ecology." History of Science 15: 189-
215.
A discussion plus annotations.

B25. Mullins, N.C., L.L. Hargens, P.K. Hecht,
and E.L. Kick

1977 "The Group Structure of Co-citation
Clusters: A Comparative Study." American Sociological Review 42 (August):
552-562.
A blockmodel analysis of two co-citation clusters in biomedicine. The
authors' preoccupation with technique,
however, blinds them to cultural and
contextual factors which do not accord
with the social structures they claim
to have detected.

B26. Nelkin, Dorothy

1977 "Scientists and Professional Responsibility: The Experience of American
Ecologists." Social Studies of Science
7 (February): 75-95.
"A study of how public demands have
affected ecologists in the United

142

States and how the latter have sought
to protect the autonomy of their discipline"[M].

B27. O'Rand, Angela M.

1977 "Professional Standing and Peer Con-
sultation Status among Biological Scientists at a Summer Research Laboratory." Social Forces 55 (June): 921-
937.

B28. Rosenberg, Charles E.

1977 "Rationalization and Reality in the
Shaping of American Agricultural Research, 1875-1914." Social Studies
of Science 7: 401-422.
"Problems in contemporary American
agricultural research have origins
in nineteenth-century economic and
social realities . . . [T]he expanding
of career options in the biological
sciences, the elaboration of new applied science disciplines, the granting of generous federal support for
extension (demonstration and education), and the increasing of support
for research all served--in a period
of institutional growth--to provide
. . . economic guidance for agricultural producers and agriculture-relat-
ed business."

B29. Small, H.G.

1977 "A Co-citation Model of a Scientific
Specialty: A Longitudinal Study of
Collagen Research." Social Studies
of Science 7 (May): 139-166.
"By analysis of successive cumulations
of citation data, clusters are ob-
served to change through time by

143

adding or dropping cited documents
. . . . [T]his methodology is applied
to the case of a biomedical specialty,
collagen research. . . . Interviews
with specialists and a questionnaire
survey are used to validate the statistical reconstruction of events ob-
tained through co-citation analysis."
This creative attempt to integrate
citation analysis with other historical and social evidence yields some
prematurely strong claims.

B30. Studer, Kenneth E.

1977 Growth and Specialization in Contemporary Biomedicine: The Case of Reverse Transcriptase. Cornell University: Unpublished doctoral dissertation.
An early version of Studer and Chubin
[B52] emphasizing eigenstructure analysis of virus cancer researchers' publications and citations.

B31. Bud, Robert F.

1978 "Strategy in American Cancer Research
after World War II: A Case Study."
Social Studies of Science 8 (November):
425-459.
"An examination of how the social lo-
cation of research on cancer influenced research strategies and contributed to the major emphasis on chemo-
therapy" [M].

B32. de Kervasdoue, Jean and Francois Billon

1978 "Development of Research and External
Influences: The Case of Cancer and
Respiratory Diseases." Social Science

144

Information 17: 735-774.
"Is research undertaken in areas where
problems exist or are discoveries made
in areas where there are solutions?"
Two cases of biomedical research and
their ties to the science policies of
France are investigated in search of
an answer.

B33.   Levitan, Karen B.

        1978 "Questioning the Relationship between
              Scientific Societies and Science Jour-
              nals." 4S Newsletter 3 (Winter): 11-
              15.
              A paper highlighting the author's un-
              published Ph.D. thesis, Functions of
              Scientific Societies: Views of Bio-
              medical Scientists, University of
              Maryland, 1976.

B34.   Manier, Edward

        1978 The Young Darwin and His Cultural Cir-
              cle. Boston: D. Reidel.

B34a.   Herbert, Sandra

        1979 "Darwin and Philosphers" (Review).
              Science 204 (18 May): 726-727.
              "In reconstructing the private philo-
              sophical world in which Darwin opera-
              ted, Manier also addresses two ques-
              tions of particular importance to
              historians and philosophers of sci-
              ence: How did Darwin choose what he
              read in philosophy? and how did his
              reading in philosophy, particularly
              respecting method, affect the form
              or content of his written work? Ma-
              nier's answer to the first question
              is only partly adequate. He suggests
              that Darwin's reading was determined

by what he terms Darwin's 'cultural circle'. . . . Manier does not make clear what external reality this circle had beyond the fact that each member of it was cited in Darwin's notes."

B34b. Ruse, Michael

1979 (Review). Philosophy of Science 46: 165-166.
"This volume, although written by a philosopher of science, is one of the first of a new series of studies in the history of modern science. . . . [It examines] the precise influences which were important in shaping the language, structure, and logic of the earliest drafts of the theory of evolution through natural selection."

B35. Nelkin, Dorothy

1978 "Threats and Promises: Negotiating the Control of Research." Daedalus 107 (Spring): 191-209.
A concise chronology and analysis of the events surrounding the voluntary moratorium on recombinant DNA research called by researchers in 1974, and its aftermath.

B36. Stepan, Nancy

1978 "The Interplay Between Socio-economic Factors and Medical Science: Yellow Fever Research, Cuba and the United States." Social Studies of Science 8: 397-423.
"This paper examines the reasons for the lag of almost twenty years between the publication in 1881 of the . . . substantially correct theory of the

146

mosquito transmission of yellow fever,
and its eventual confirmation . . .
in 1900."

B37. Allen, Garland

1979 "The Transformation of a Science: T.
H. Morgan and the Emergence of a New
American Biology." Pp. 173-210 in A.
Oleson and J. Voss (eds.), [G54].
" . . . from a largely descriptive to
an increasingly experimental science
. . ."

B38. Chubin, D.E. and K.E. Studer

1979 "Knowledge and Structures of Scientific Growth: Measurement of a Cancer
Problem Domain." Scientometrics 1
(January): 171-193.
"An examination of various measures
of the growth and structure of a research area in the light of interpretive analysis of the cognitive content
of the area" [M]. For a more comprehensive treatment, see chapters 5 and
6 of Studer and Chubin [B52].

B39. Fleck, Ludwik

1979 Genesis and Development of a Scientific Fact. F. Bradley and T.J. Trenn
(trans.), T.J. Trenn and R.K. Merton
(eds.). Chicago: University of Chicago Press.

B39a. Rosenkrantz, Barbara Gutmann

1981 "Reflecktions" (Review). Isis 72:
96-99.
"Fleck examines the relationship between thought and experience in the

construction of scientific facts in
order to clarify the origins and development of scientific knowledge.
He turns to . . . the successive re-
formulations of the concept of syphi-
lis over five hundred years, during
which socially and medically accepted
criteria for diagnosis of venereal
disease interacted. . . ."

B40. Gillespie, Brendan, Dave Eva, and Ron
      Johnston

      1979 "Carcinogenic Risk Assessment in the
            United States and Great Britain: The
            Case of Aldrin/Dieldrin." Social
            Studies of Science 9 (August): 265-
            301.
            Two pesticides, Aldrin and Dieldrin,
            were judged to be carcinogenic in the
            U.S. but not in Britain, although the
            same evidence was available to public
            authorities in both countries. This
            article shows that "the different na-
            tional resources and evaluations of
            dread diseases such as cancer have
            affected the availability, and type,
            of expertise for the assessment of
            carcinogenic risk. In both countries,
            toxicology has been, historically,
            most closely associated with the pri-
            vate sector and the government agen-
            cies responsible for the regulation
            of toxic hazards. This has been rein-
            forced by the failure of toxicology,
            as a scientific field, to develop a
            unique identity within national uni-
            versity systems. Still, the greater
            resources and commitment to health
            protection in the U.S. has resulted
            in the development of a larger, more
            diverse biomedical research system,

in which more basic research institutions, independent of regulatory-re-
gulatee interests, operate." A cogent
case of scientific rationality tested
in the political arena.

B41.   Hackett, Edward J.

1979   Social and Cultural Influences on Con-
       temporary Biomedical Science: A Case
       Study of Friend Virus Research. Cor-
       nell University: Unpublished doctoral
       dissertation.
       Uses a bibliometric approach for un-
       raveling a basic biomedical science
       specialty.

B42.   Jordanova, Ludmilla J. and Roy S. Porter
       (eds.)

1979   Images of the Earth: Essays in the
       History of the Environmental Sciences.
       Chalfont St. Giles: British Society
       for the History of Science Monographs.

B43.   Kohler, Robert E.

1979   "Medical Reform and Biomedical Science:
       Biochemistry--A Case Study." Pp. 27-
       66 in M.J. Vogel and C.E. Rosenberg
       (eds.), The Therapeutic Revolution.
       Essays in the Social History of Ameri-
       can Medicine, Philadelphia: University
       of Pennsylvania Press.
       Of all the biomedical disciplines,
       biochemistry "is the one least direct-
       ly involved in clinical practice.
       Morever, its establishment as a sepa-
       rate discipline was an immediate re-
       sult of the reforms in medical educa-
       tion in the 1900s. Its history illus-
       trates how a science can lend symbolic
       or political significance to a medical

reform movement . . ."

B44.   Judson, Horace Freeland

1979   The Eighth Day of Creation: The Mak-
        ers of the Revolution in Biology.
        New York: Simon and Schuster.
        Yet another account, this time by a
        journalist, of the discovery of the
        structure of DNA.

B44a.   Bearman, David

1980   "Disciplines, Disciples, and the Mak-
        ing of Biology" (Review). Isis 71:
        140-142.
        "Unfettered by assumptions about what
        he should see in biology, Judson finds
        and documents an extraordinary variety
        of theorizing. . . . In an afterword,
        Judson advances a thematic explanation
        . . . . [which] challenges, quite le-
        gitimately, the received historiogra-
        phy of molecular biology . . ."

1979   Latour, Bruno and Steve Woolgar

        See [L12].

B45.   Lenoir, Timothy

1979   "Quantitative Foundations for the
        Sociology of Science: On Linking
        Blockmodeling with Co-citation Analy-
        sis." Social Studies of Science 9:
        455-480.
        The author presents a "review of re-
        cent investigations of reverse tran-
        scriptase," but admits that "no co-
        citation study has yet been attempted
        which provides a detailed and fine-
        grained analysis of the cognitive
        structure of reverse transcriptase."

150

It seems premature, therefore, to conclude that block-modeling delineates
social groups that possess a common
cognitive orientation. The author
leans heavily on published papers by
Mullins et al. [B25] and Chubin and
Studer [B38], and on an unpublished
paper by Chubin et al. [G32]. That
Lenoir's "discussion paper" appeared
months before the Studer and Chubin
[B52] monograph on reverse transcriptase renders his attempt at best incom-
plete and at worst a misrepresentation
--with and without attribution--of
various source documents. Shoddy scholarship is abundantly evident here.

B46. Levitan, Karen B.

1979 "Scientific Societies and Their Journals: Biomedical Scientists Assess the
Relationship." Social Studies of Science 9: 393-400.

B47. Rossiter, Margaret W.

1979 "The Organization of the Agricultural
Sciences." Pp. 211-248 in A. Oleson
and J. Voss (eds.), [G54].
An overview of the major subfields of
agriculture in the period 1880 to 1920,
including economic entomology; horti-
culture, breeding, and genetics; animal nutrition and husbandry; plant and
animal pathology; agronomy and regional
development; and soil science.

B48. Webster, A.J.

1979 "Scientific Controversy and Socio-Cog-
nitive Metonymy: The Case of Acupunc-

ture." Pp. 121-137 in R. Wallis (ed.),
[G56].
"A study of the reception of acupunc-
ture by the Western research community"
[M].

B49. Yoxen, Edward J.

1979 "Where Does Schrodinger's What is Life?
Belong in the History of Molecular Biology?" History of Science 17: 17-52.
"[M]olecular biology has coincided with
and indeed has been partly responsible
for, a fundamental transformation in
the way biological questions are conceived. What is Life? . . . offers a
vantage point on which to stand, just
outside the current conceptual framework, to perceive the change which has
taken place."

Latour, Bruno

1980 See [L17].

McKegney, Doug

1980 See [L18].

B50. Hargens, Lowell L., Nicholas C. Mullins,
and Pamela K. Hecht

1980 "Research Areas and Stratification Processes in Science." Social Studies of
Science 10: 55-74.
In this analysis of two biomedical
clusters---Australia antigen and reverse transcriptase--the authors again
apply the cocitation-blockmodel methodology [Mullins et al., B25], tied to
a center-periphery interpretation, in
an effort to relate "research area

structure" to "stratification processes." With such methodological standardization and indifference to intellectual content, as well as to cultural
and political context, it is no sur-
prise that the outcome is both flawed
and misleading.

B51. Roll-Hansen, Nils

1980 "The Controversy Between Biometricians
and Mendelians: A Test Case for the
Sociology of Scientific Knowledge."
Social Science Information 19: 501-
517.
In this re-examination of a controversy
the author concludes "that the dispute
was solved in full accordance with the
rationalist view of science. With respect to the scientific progress that
was made, external factors played a
subsidiary role. . . . I have tried
to show how Barnes' and MacKenzie's
[e.g., S45] use of this controversy as
a case against rationalism is based on
historical misunderstandings." It is
implied that thus far the "strong programme" has flunked the test (but see
Barnes and Shapin [G49]).

B52. Studer, K.E. and D.E. Chubin

1980 The Cancer Mission: Social Contexts
of Biomedical Research. Beverly
Hills: Sage.

B52a. Yoxen, Edward J.

1981 "Confluence in Research" (Review).
Science 211 (23 January): 378-379.

"One of the problems . . . is that
[the authors] seem to be trying to

address two peer groups at once. Almost certainly any cancer researchers reading the book will find much of the epistemological discussion obsure and convoluted . . . [T]he book represents a useful effort to combine a number of different approaches to a complex problem."

B52b. Bruer, John T.

1981 (Review). Scientometrics 3 (July): 335-337.
"As the authors argue, the pre-eminence of social factors in explanations of scientific progress and the concomitant relativism force questions of science policy into the framework . . . of possible social constraints on a semi-autonomous cognitive system. . . . To remedy these shortcomings, the authors develop their own confluence theory of scientific development. . . which they admit may be suited only to biological sciences. . . . [Still], there appears to be a gap between the theoretical framework and the analysis of the literature."

B52c. Thaler, Robert

1981 (Review). 4S Newsletter 6 (Winter): 12-15.
This "review" awaits the enterprising reader. (Further annotation would be self-serving.)

B52d. Holtzman, Eric and Sally Guttmacher

1981 (Review). Contemporary Sociology 10 (September): 674-676.
"One special merit [of the book] is

154

that it concerns science that is both
very recent and quite important. Another is that it deals with modern biology, a neglected field by comparison
with modern physics or evolutionary
theory. The writing is often clumsy,
but not unbearably so. Sociologists,
take warning, however: you may need a
biologist to help you interpret large
segments of the presentation."

B53. Travis, G.D.L.

1980 "On the Construction of Creativity:
The 'Memory Transfer' Phenomenon and
the Importance of Being Earnest." Pp.
165-193 in Knorr et al. (eds.) [L15].

"In this paper, I will examine part
of the climate of opinion surrounding
the reception of [memory transfer] . . .
including violations of tacit rules
for doing science . . ."

B54. Travis, G.D.L.

1980 "Some Aspects of the Nonestablishment
of Memory Transfer." Presented at Conference on Scientific Establishments and
Hierarchies, Oxford University (July).
Drawing on a case study of "memory
transfer," a long-running controversy
in neurobiology, the author discusses
a "set of experiments, theoretical notions and scientists which became
identified as a research area having
a distinctive approach" (see Travis
[B53] for an earlier installment).

B55. Yoxen, Edward J.

1980 "Giving Life a New Meaning: The Rise

of the Molecular Biology Establishment." Presented at Conference on Scientific Establishments and Hierarchies
(July), Oxford University (forthcoming
in Sociology of the Sciences, Vol. 6).

"[T]he emergence of biotechnology is
a political drama in which some life
scientists are learning to assume new
public roles, whilst some remain committed to the more traditional parts."
The author's present focus is "on the
conditions that led to the consolidation of molecular biology and the power of molecular biologists within national scientific establishments. . . .
It is precisely the claim to be able
to conceptualise and act upon the most
fundamental constitutive processes of
life . . . that has conferred upon molecular biology its power in particular
social conditions." This paper continues the author's formidable research
initiated in his 1978 Ph.D. thesis
(Cambridge University) entitled, "The
Social Impact of Molecular Biology"
and Yoxen [B48].

B56. Aaronson, Naomi

1981 "Vitamins: A Contextualist Account of
a Scientific Concept." Presented at
Annual Meeting, American Sociological
Association, Toronto (August).

B57. Frank, Robert G., Jr.

1981 Harvey and the Oxford Physiologists.
Scientific Ideas and Social Interaction. Berkeley: University of Cali-
fornia Press.

B57a.　Hall, Thomas S.

　　　　1981　"A 17th Century Scientific Community"
　　　　　　　(Review).　Science 213 (31 July):
　　　　　　　532-533.
　　　　　　　"His [Frank's] purpose is to show the
　　　　　　　interplay between the flow of ideas
　　　　　　　about respiration at the time and
　　　　　　　the conditions, or context, that per-
　　　　　　　mitted ideas to flow. . . . The web
　　　　　　　of interaction spreads as he traces
　　　　　　　its involvement of a dozen 'major'
　　　　　　　and a score or more 'minor' scientists
　　　　　　　and peripherally participant 'vir-
　　　　　　　tuosi.' . . . What we have in Frank's
　　　　　　　book if taken as a whole is as enter-
　　　　　　　prising, engaging, and enlightening
　　　　　　　an example of historical interpreta-
　　　　　　　tion as this reviewer has recently
　　　　　　　read."

　　　Knorr, K.D.

　　　1981　See [L25].

　　　Lynch, Michael

　　　1981　See [L27].

SOCIAL SCIENCE: History, Philosophy, and Any "Self"
            Study of a Social Science Discipline
            or Specialty

S01.   Cole, Stephen

       1972 "Continuity and Institutionalization
             in Science: A Case Study of Failure."
             Pp. 23-129 in A. Oberschall (ed.),
             The Establishment of Empirical Socio-
             logy. New York: Harper and Row.

S02.   Garvey, William D. and Belver C. Griffith

       1972 "Communication and Information Pro-
             cessing within Scientific Disciplines:
             Empirical Findings for Psychology."
             Information Storage and Retrieval 8:
             123-136.
             "Scientific disciplines can be regarded
             as social devices which have, as one
             function, the analysis and reduction
             of raw information to assimilated know-
             ledge . . . transmitted through pro-
             fessional training. Data on informa-
             tion flow in psychology reveal a
             lengthy series of disseminations to
             various audiences."

S03.   Krantz, David L.

       1972 "Schools and Systems: The Mutual Iso-
             lation of Operant and Non-Operant Psy-
             chology as a Case Study." Journal of
             the History of Behavioral Sciences
             8: 86-102.
             "The mean percentage of self-citation
             is used as an index of the isolation
             of operant and non-operant schools in
             psychology" [I].

S04.   Oberschall, Anthony (ed.)

       1972   The Establishment of Empirical Soci-
               ology. New York: Harper and Row.

S05.   Deleted.

S06.   Reynolds, L.T. and C.L. McCart

       1972   "The Institutional Basis of Theoreti-
               cal Diversity." Sociological Focus
               5: 16-39.
               A study of orientations within symbolic
               interactionism.

S07.   Stehr, Nico and Lyle E. Larson

       1972   "The Rise and Decline of Areas of
               Specialization." The American Soci-
               ologist 7 (August): 3,5,6.
               "Examines changes in areas of specia-
               lization in sociology. Results of a
               1970 questionnaire survey of a sample
               of American Sociological Association
               members are compared to specialty
               lists from 1959 and 1950 studies.
               The data show some shift in rank order
               of specialties. Rankings of areas of
               specialization by age groups of socio-
               logists show that areas of interest
               tend to be retained over time, which
               suggests that differences specific to
               generations of sociologists may per-
               sist. Change of specialties is slight
               among the youngest and oldest socio-
               logists; the largest number of chan-
               ges occur among sociologists in the
               middle years bracket" [P].

S08.   Thackray, Arnold and Robert K. Merton

       1972   "On Discipline Building: The Paradoxes
               of George Sarton." Isis 63: 473-495.

               "[T]he creation of a cognitive iden-
               tity is only one facet of the insti-
               tutionalization of a field of learn-

ing. A parallel set of shifts . . .
revolves around the creation of a
professional identity for the new
enterprise . . . The limits of George
Sarton's influence on the history of
science reveal by default how the cognitive identity of a discipline is a
matter of theoretical orientation and
worldview as well as tools and techniques. His inability to engineer
the careers and train the disciples
who would create a professional identity for his subject also demonstrates
how much this latter aspect of disci-
pline-building depends on factors beyond the control of any individual."

S09. Baker, A.R.H.

1973 "A Cliometric on the Citation Structure of Historical Geography." Professional Geographer 25: 347-349.

S10. Barber, Bernard

1973 "Research on Research on Human Subjects: Problems of Access to a Power-
ful Profession." Social Problems 21
(Summer): 103-112.

S11. Biglan, Anthony

1973 "Relationships between Subject Matter
Characteristics and the Structure and
Output of University Departments."
Journal of Applied Psychology 57: 204-
213.
An attempt to typologize fields, e.g.,
as hard-soft, life-nonlife, pure-ap-
plied.

S12.   Clark, Terry

       1973   Prophets and Patrons: The French Uni-
              versity and the Emergence of the So-
              cial Sciences. Cambridge: Harvard
              University Press.
              A social history of institutionaliza-
              tion.

S13.   French, Richard and Michael Gross

       1973   "A Survey of North American Graduate
              Students in the History of Science
              1970-71." Science Studies 3: 161-
              179.
              Results of a mail survey show that
              the most popular fields of interest
              are 19th-century life sciences, 19th
              century physics, and social history
              of science. Far and away the most
              widely read journal is Isis.

S14.   Krantz, D.L. and L. Wiggins

       1973   "Personal and Impersonal Channels of
              Recruitment in the Growth of Theory."
              Human Development 16: 133-156.
              "Recruitment of followers to a scien-
              tific theory occurs through at least
              two channels--personal and imper-
              sonal." Focusing on the theories of
              four psychologists--Tolman, Hull,
              Spence, and Skinner--the author finds
              "that while impersonal recruitment
              produces the greatest number of fol-
              lowers, personal recruitment increases
              and maintains affiliation." Evidence
              that supports the supposition that
              "personal influence" operates in
              science, too. For more, see Campbell
              [S48].

S15.   Mullins, Nicholas C.

        1973   Theory and Theory Groups in Contem-
                porary American Sociology. New York:
                Harper and Row.

S15a.   Truzzi, Marcello

        1975   (Review). Contemporary Sociology 4
                (May): 223-225.
                "Basically, Mullins has attempted to
                apply a four-stage model of group de-
                velopment [see B01]. . . to study so-
                ciologists. The four stages (the nor-
                mal, network, cluster, and specialty
                phases) are presented as non-exclusive
                but basically sequential patterns
                through which scientific group struc-
                tures pass. He then examines eight
                sociological 'theory groups' . . .
                [but]actually presents us merely with
                a conceptual scaffolding from which
                to examine his groups' organizational
                structures and changes . . ." The
                book reminds us that "some members of
                the discipline will have more impact
                than others because of their social
                position, quite aside from the intel-
                lectual validity of their ideas."

S15b.   Oromanor, Mark

        1975   (Review). Contemporary Sociology 4
                (May): 225-226.
                The book examines, via a "structura-
                list" model, "'how, over time, groups
                of social theorists form, grow, and
                then cease to exist.' These trans-
                formations are 'assumed to be self-
                regulating--that is, not requiring
                explanations based on individuals'
                personalities, general characteristics

of American society or the intellectual history of sociology.' . . .
The structuralists, centering around
Harrison C. White, form one of Mullins' emerging active theory groups.
What better way to get the word to
other sociologists than to conduct a
structuralist analysis of sociological groups?"

S16.   Mullins, N.C.

       1973   "The Development of Specialties in
              Social Science: The Case of Ethnome-
              thodology." Science Studies 3: 245-
              273.

S17.   Schmitt, R.L.

       1973   "'Knowledge Crystallization' in the
              Reference Group Literature." Presented
              at Annual Meeting, American Sociolo-
              gical Association, New York (August).

S18.   Spreitzer, Elmer and Larry J. Reynolds

       1973   "Patterning in Citations: An Analysis
              of References to George Herbert Mead."
              Sociological Focus 6: 71-82.

S19.   Weimer, Walter B. and David S. Palermo

       1973   "Paradigms and Normal Science in Psy-
              chology." Science Studies 3: 211-
              244.
              Examines "both the claim that psycho-
              logy is susceptible to analysis in
              Kuhn's terms . . . [and argues] against
              the tendency to construe any concep-
              tion and methodology of science as a
              template."

S20.   Carroll, Michael P.

1974   "The Effects of the Functionalist Pa-
        radigm upon the Perception of Ethno-
        graphic data." Philosophy of the
        Social Sciences 4: 65-74.
        " . . . looking only at topics inclu-
        ded in ethnographic reports both be-
        fore and after the rise of functiona-
        lism [in social anthropology], do de-
        scriptions of these typics systemati-
        cally differ as a result of the shift
        . . .?" Yes, but the correlations
        are not statistically significant
        (and inappropriate for testing the
        hypothesis anyway).

S21.   Duncan, S.S.

1974   "The Isolation of Scientific Disco-
        very: Indifference and Resistance
        to a New Idea." Science Studies 4:
        109-134.
        This paper "concerns the reception
        of spatial diffusion theory by re-
        searchers in human geography . . ."
        An impressive synthesis of biblio-
        metric, network, and other data never-
        theless leads the author to conclude:
        "The relationship between the 'core
        and scatter' and 'normal and crisis'
        models of science remains unclear.
        Both postulate cores of individuals
        (in one model they possess prestige
        and influence, in the other opposing
        paradigms), and both models depend
        on the concept of an articulating
        flow of information. The two models
        may describe the same phenomenon from
        different viewpoints."

164

S22.   Lipsey, Mark

        1974   "Psychology: Preparadigmatic, Post-
                paradigmatic, Misparadigmatic?" Sci-
                ence Studies 4: 406-410.
                A comment on Weimer and Palermo's
                [S19] "argument that psychology has
                had a paradigm (behaviourism) and a
                revolution (cognitive psychology), and
                thus is indeed paradigmatic . . ."

S23.   Mitroff, Ian I.

        1974   "On Doing Empirical Philosophy of Sci-
                ence: A Case Study in the Social Psy-
                chology of Research." Philosophy of
                the Social Sciences 4: 183-196.
                "In sum, I think Kuhn was right in
                his basic appeal to social psychology
                and history as one way of doing phi-
                losophy of science. . . . To para-
                phrase Kant, we would not have found
                continuity, or its absence, in science
                unless we had not first put it there
                ourselves."

S24.   Quarantelli, E.L. and J.M. Weller

        1974   "The Structural Problem of a Sociolo-
                gical Specialty: Collective Behavior's
                Lack of a Critical Mass." The Ameri-
                can Sociologist 9 (May): 59-68.
                Presents the results of a mail survey
                of North American specialists in col-
                lective behavior.

S25.   Stehr, Nico

        1974   "Paradigmatic Crystallization: Pat-
                terns of Interrelations among Areas
                of Competence in Sociology." Social
                Science Information 13: 119-137.

S26.   Stehr, Nico
        1974   "Factors in the Development of Multi-

paradigm Disciplines: The Case of
Sociology." Journal of the History
of the Behavioral Sciences: 172-188.

This paper analyzes factors--cogni-
tive, organizational, and demogra-
phic--in the development of two sociological specialties: marriage and
the family, and political sociology.
Differential rates of growth in membership are related to the continuity
of cognitive and structural characteristics of the specialties.

S27. Cole, Jonathan R. and Harriet A. Zuckerman

1975   "The Emergence of a Scientific Specialty: The Self-exemplifying Case
of the Sociology of Science." Pp.
139-174 in Lewis A. Coser (ed.), The
Idea of Social Structure: Papers in
Honor of Robert K. Merton. New York:
Harcourt, Brace.
"A systematic analysis of certain
aspects of the development of the
Mertonian School in the sociology of
science. Special attention is given
to parameters of growth [and] cognitive development as revealed by patterns of citation and identification
of 'influentials'" [M]. As informa-
tive for what it omits as for what
it glorifies.

S28. Cole, Stephen

1975   "The Growth of Scientific Knowledge:
Theories of Deviance as a Case Stu-
dy." Pp. 175-220 in L.A. Coser (ed.),
The Idea of Social Structure. New
York: Harcourt, Brace.
An analysis of references to Merton's
work on social structure and anomie.

166

S29. Mullins, N.C.

1975 "New Causal Theory: An Elite Specialty in Social Science." History of Political Economy 7 (Winter): 499-529.

S30. Ritzer, George

1975 "Sociology: A Multiple Paradigm Science." The American Sociologist 10 (August): 156-167.
An application, a la Friedrichs' A Sociology of Sociology, of Kuhn's theory to sociology. Ritzer discerns three paradigms competing for hegemony within the discipline as a whole as well as within virtually every subarea within sociology": the "social facts paradigm," the "social definition" paradigm, and the "social behavior paradigm." For more, see Ritzer [S31, S51*].

S31. Ritzer, George

1975 Sociology: A Multiple Paradigm Science. Boston: Allyn and Bacon.

S32. Szacki, Jerzy

1975 "'Schools' in Sociology." Social Science Information 12: 173-182.
What does 'school' denote, connote, and promote in the history of sociology?

S33. Wagner, H.R.

1975 "Sociologists of Phenomenological Orientations: Their Place in American Sociology." The American Sociologist 10 (August): 179-186.

A survey of North American phenomeno-
logists.

S34. Wynne, Brian

1975   "The Rhetoric of Consensus Politics:
        Critical Review of Technology Assess-
        ment." Research Policy 4: 108-158.
        Technology assessment as an emergent
        specialty, with "dangerous" tendencies
        as a policy tool, is examined.

S35. Harwood, Jonathan

1976   "The Race-Intelligence Controversy:
        A Sociological Approach. I. Profes-
        sional Factors." Social Studies of
        Science 6: 369-394.
        An internalist interpretation of the
        controversy between hereditarians
        and environmentalists. For an exami-
        nation of the adversaries' social
        and political commitments, see Har-
        wood [S38].

S36. MacKenzie, Donald

1976   "Eugenics in Britain." Social Stu-
        dies of Science 6: 499-532.
        The paper traces the relation of eu-
        genic ideology and the development
        of mathematical statistics to "the
        differential appeal of eugenics to
        the various social classes and occu-
        pational groups in Britain."

S37. McVaugh, Michael and Seymour H. Mauskopf

1976   "J.B. Rhine's Extra-Sensory Percep-
        tion and its background in psychical
        research." Isis 67: 161-189.

The authors offer qualified support
for the view that Extra-Sensory Perception was the paradigmatic work
for parapsychology.

S38. Harwood, Jonathan

1977 "The Race-Intelligence Controversy:
A Sociological Approach. II. 'Exter-
nal' Factors." Social Studies of
Science 7: 1-30.

S39. Merton, Robert K.

1977 "The Sociology of Science: An Episodic Memoir." Pp. 3-141 in R.K. Merton and J. Gaston (eds.), The Sociology of Science in Europe. Carbon-
dale: Southern Illinois University
Press.
A masterful essay by a founding father
of the specialty known as "sociology
of science." It begins, appropriately
enough, with kudos to Derek Price for
adopting and extending the 17th-cen-
tury concept of "invisible colleges"
and proceeds to a rendition of the
specialty's institutionalization.
Sketches of precursors such as Sarton
and Popper are capped by an affection-
ate 38-page intellectual history of
Kuhn. An inventory of "specialty-
specific research procedures"--proso-
pography, content analysis, citation
analysis, and the "science indicators"
enterprise--concludes this rewarding
"oral history."

S39a. Oromaner, Mark

1978 (Review). 4S Newsletter 3 (Fall):
44-47.

A critique of Merton's episodic memoir and especially his biography of Kuhn. Oromaner challenges the "assumption that all of the talent necessary for the development of any particular field is possessed by the students and faculty of America's elite institutions." I second the challenge.

Spiegel-Roesing, Ina

1977 See [C17].

S40. Toulmin, Stephen

1977 "From Form to Function: Philosophy and History of Science in the 1950s and Now." Daedalus 106 (Summer): 143-162.
A social history that probes the reasons for former divergences and recent convergences between these two specialties.

S41. Ben-David, Joseph

1978 "Emergence of National Traditions in the Sociology of Science: The United States and Great Britain." Pp. 197-218 in J. Gaston (ed.), Sociology of Science. San Francisco: Jossey-Bass.

The author offers a myopic and somewhat outdated perspective.

S42. Farr, Robert M.

1978 "On the Varieties of Social Psychology: An Essay on the Relationships between Psychology and Other Social Sciences." Social Science Information

170

17: 503-525.
The author considers three traditions
of social psychology: American symbolic interactionism, Durkheim-in-
spired French research on "representa-
tions sociales," and experimental social psychology.

S43.   Freidheim, Elizabeth A.

       1978 "A Quantitative Procedure for Clas-
             sifying the Content of Theory-Research
             Works." The Sociological Quarterly
             19 (Spring): 234-252.
             A content analysis of sociological
             themes that overcomes some of the
             weaknesses of Ritzer's [S31] approach.

S44.   Gusfield, Joseph R.

       1978 "Historical Problematics and Sociolo-
             gical Fields: American Liberalism
             and the Study of Social Movements."
             Research in Sociology of Knowledge,
             Sciences and Art 1:121-149.
             "My emphasis here is on ways in which
             political and social perspectives
             and events, external to sociological
             theory and research, have played a
             decisive role in the internal logic
             of this corner of social science. . . .
             Where social movements will be in
             the next decade will depend to a great
             measure on what history has hidden
             in its next act."

S45.   MacKenzie, Donald

       1978 "Statistical Theory and Social In-
             terests: A Case Study." Social Stu-
             dies of Science 8: 35-83.

"Discusses the influence of social
and ideological issues on the development of the mathematical theory of statistics in Britain. Controversy over
the measurement of statistical association is seen as a reflection of
different goals and cognitive interests of two groups of statisti-
cians: those committed to eugenics
research and those with no special
commitments." [P].

S46. Norton, Bernard

1978 "Karl Pearson and Statistics: The
Social Origins of Scientific Innovation." Social Studies of Science
8: 3-34.

S47. Westrum, Ron

1978 "Science and Social Intelligence a-
bout Anomalies: The Case of Meteo-
rites." Social Studies of Science
8 (November): 461-493.
"The present paper is an attempt to
examine the anomaly reporting processes which led to the scientific
recognition of the reality of meteo-
rites in the eighteenth century . . . .
The treatment of reports . . . is
further shown to be related to the
scientific community's concerns about
protecting its internal processes
from external interference."

S48. Campbell, Donald T.

1979 "A Tribal Model of the Social System
Vehicle Carrying Scientific Knowledge." Knowledge: Creation, Diffusion, Utilization 1 (December): 181-

201.
Part 2 of a larger study of major
learning theorists of the 1930s and
1940s (see Krantz and Wiggins [S14]).
This paper focuses on Edward Tolman
and Kenneth Spence, "selected for
maximum contrast on both leadership
effectiveness and personality and leadership style. . . . Scientific knowledge is maintained by a social system vehicle whose social structure
maintenance requirements are prere-
quisite to the improvement, preserva-
tion, and transmission of a valid model of (for example) the physical
world. These social structural re-
quisites make sciences, and theoretical schools within science, similar
to other self-perpetuating belief communities, the common characteristics
of which are epitomized as 'tribal'
in this essay."

S49.   Collins, H.M. and T.J. Pinch

1979   "The Construction of the Paranormal:
       Nothing Unscientific is Happening."
       Pp. 237-270 in R. Wallis (ed.), [G56].
       A detailed discussion of the tactics
       employed by adversaries in the strug-
       gle to establish parapsychology as a
       scientific discipline.

S50.   Eckberg, D.L. and L. Hill, Jr.

1979   "The Paradigm Concept and Sociology:
       A Critical Review." American Sociolo-
       gical Review 44 (December): 925-937.

       "The thesis of this paper contends
       that many sociologists who have at-
       tempted to apply Kuhn's argument in
       analyzing the status of sociology have

misunderstood, or have refused to accept the central meaning of his paradigm concept. . . . [W]e argue that sociology has relatively few exemplars, lacks a clear-cut puzzle-solving tradition, and tends to operate from discipline-wide perspectives. In this regard, sociology is not a mature science; attempts to treat it as such within Kuhn's framework are misdirected." An otherwise savvy sociological critique perpetuates the time-worn hegemony-of-the-natural-sciences ideology.

S51.* Ritzer, George

1981 "Paradigm Analysis in Sociology: Clarifying the Issues." American Sociological Review 46 (April): 245-248.

S52.* Eckberg, D.L. and L. Hill, Jr.

1981 "Clarifying Confusions about Paradigms: A Reply to Ritzer." American Sociological Review 46 (April): 248-252.

Ritzer: "Eckberg and Hill delineate four characteristics of an exemplar; we can extend their discussion by enumerating a parallel set of characteristics of disciplinary matrices . . . [which are more useful] for understanding the metatheoretical status of sociology, both presently and in terms of its immediate future." Eckberg and Hill: "By constructing 'paradigms on the basis of a priori categories,' Ritzer totally misses the community nature of paradigms. . . . Now, Ritzer has merely expanded his categories, adding crosscutting dimensions. Is this technique really sup-

174

posed to get at the core of sociology? Does it get at any specific ongoing discourse? Can it isolate communities of thought? We think not."

Verdict: Eckberg and Hill are correct
in stressing the community basis of
paradigms. That is central to Kuhn's
theory. Efforts to impose paradigm
status on a body of literature or its
authors, in other words, are seriously
misguided. To term such efforts "metatheoretical" is an abstraction with
no corresponding social reality.

S53.   Farkas, Janos (ed.)

1979   Sociology of Science and Research.
       Budapest: Akademiai Kiado.
       This volume contains 34 papers orga-
       nized into 4 parts, including 16 on
       "The Sociology of the Research Pro-
       cess." Based on a sociology of sci-
       ence conference held in Budapest in
       1977.

S54.   Freidheim, Elizabeth A.

1979   "An Empirical Comparison of Ritzer's
       Paradigms and Similar Metatheories:
       A Research Note." Social Forces 58-
       59-66.
       The author asks "whether there are
       empirically identifiable metatheore-
       tical perspectives in sociology, and
       to what degree these perspectives,
       assuming they exist, form a closed
       theoretical world." She finds, based
       on a multidimensional scaling of 24
       works identified and classified by
       Ritzer, that "theory tendencies do
       exist in sociology, but not as well
       marked paradigm views . . . . [W]e

cannot use his data as evidence of
profound, near total cognitive divi-
sions in sociology."

S55.* Freidheim, Elizabeth A.

    1980 "An Empirical Comparison of Ritzer's
Paradigms and Similar Metatheories:
Response to Harper, Sylvester, and
Walczak." Social Forces 59 (December): 518-520.
" . . . shifts from one theory type
to another do suggest that disputes
may be more political than substantive at the core."

S56. Mitcham, Carl and Jim Grote

    1979 "Technology Assessment: Supplementary
Bibliography." Research in Philoso-
phy and Technology 2: 357-370.
"One problem in TA is that it can refer both to a technical discipline
and to a general attempt by society
to come to terms with the influence
of technological change. . . . TA
readily shades into studies of the
relationship between technology and
society, economics, and environmental
ethics--topics which have been given
only limited attention in this bibliography." Excellent annotations; coverage extends from 1967 to 1978 arranged in alphabetical order of authors' surnames.

S57. Pinch, Trevor J.

    1979 "Normal Explanations of the Paranor-
mal: The Demarcation Problem and Fraud
in Parapsychology." Social Studies
of Science 9 (August): 329-348.

176

"[I]t is possible to turn the demarcation arguments which have been used against 'pseudo-sciences,' such as parapsychology, against the fraud hypothesis--which is the principal normal counter-explanation. . . . It is argued that the rejection of parapsychology rests on cultural differences which demarcation criteria serve to legitimate." For more, see Pinch and Collins [S58].

S58.   Pinch, T.J. and H. M. Collins

        1979   "Is Anti-science Not Science? The Case of Parapsychology." Pp. 221-250 in H. Nowotny and H. Rose (eds.), Counter-Movements in the Sciences. Vol. 3. Dordrecht: D. Reidel.

S59.   Reed, Edward S. and Rebecca K. Jones

        1979   "James Gibson's Ecological Revolution in Psychology." Philosophy of the Social Sciences 9: 189-204. Perception and perceptual development research versus the "old regime."

S60.   Rossini, Frederick A.

        1979   "Technology Assessment: A New Type of Science?" Research in Philosophy and Technology 2: 341-355. The answer is a resounding yes, as Wynne [S34] feared in 1975. Also see Dylander [S68] and Mitcham and Grote [S56].

S61.   Small, Henry G. and Diana Crane

        1979   "Specialties and Disciplines in Science and Social Science: An Examina-

tion of Their Structure using Citation Indexes." <u>Scientometrics</u> 1:
445-461.
"Examines the development of knowledge in the social sciences, and
makes comparisons with natural science. Co-citation analysis of the
<u>Social Science Citation Index</u> for
the period 1972-1974 identifies over
1200 research clusters. The home
discipline (economics, psychology,
sociology) of a cluster is determined
by its journals of publication. Citation patterns in the social science
disciplines are compared with those
in high energy physics" [P]. Too
much standardization on methodological grounds for me.

S62.   Snizek, William F., Ellsworth R. Fuhrman,
and Michael K. Miller (eds.)

1979   <u>Contemporary Issues in Theory and
Research</u>: A Metasociological Perspective. Westport, Conn.: Greenwood.
Some elders of mainstream sociological traditions recount their suc-
cesses. For an exception, see Wiley
[S65].

S63.   Stark, Jerry A., Larry T. Reynolds, and
Leonard Lieberman

1979   "The Social Basis of Conceptual Di-
versity: A Case Study of the Concept
of 'race' in Physical Anthropology."
<u>Research in Sociology of Knowledge,
Sciences and Art</u> 2: 87-99.
Mannheim's "modes of thought" concept
is applied to the debate over race
among physical anthropologists.
"Those who hold differing viewpoints

of this concept are of demonstrably different social derivation."

S64.   Stehr, Nico and Anthony Simmons

        1979   "The Diversity of Modes of Discourse and the Development of Sociological Knowledge." Zeitschrift fur Allgemeine Wissenschaftstheorie 10: 141-161.
        "This paper presents an analysis of the structure of contemporary sociological knowledge in terms of a theory of scientific discourse. The concept of 'discourse' is introduced as a theoretical refinement of . . . 'paradigm' and is applied to the classes of knowledge claims of the natural and social sciences. . . . A classification is . . . proposed which identifies three modes of sociological discourse: natural, technical and formal." The authors' proclaimed neutrality of discourse as a description of "cognitive structure . . . that contains no implicit theory of scientific development" must be questioned.

S65.   Wiley, Norbert

        1979   "The Rise and Fall of Dominating Theories in American Sociology." Pp. 47-79 in W.E. Snizek et al. (eds.), [S62].
        A politically astute intellectual history.

S66.   Chua, Beng-Huat

        1980   "The Structure of the Contemporary Sociological Problematic: A Foucaul-

tian View." The American Sociologist 15 (May): 82-93.
This essay demonstrates that different theoretical perspectives in
sociology "are divergent developments
that emerge from the same epistemological site produced by the discon-
tinuous changes in the conception of
the function of language and of representation at the close of the
eighteenth century." The resolution
of theoretical differences, therefore, may lie not in synthesis "because they gain their grounds of co-
presence precisely in their differences." Other linguistic analyses
of sociological pluralism are found
in Stehr and Simmons [S64] and Stehr
[S73].

S67.   Collins, Randall and Sal Restivo

1980   "Sociologists in the Land of 'History
of Mathematics:' A Tale of Two Theorists." Presented at Joint Meeting
of Science/Technology Studies Societies (4S, HSS, PSA, SHOT), Toronto
(October).
The authors' "explorations in the
comparative history of mathematics
have been carried out with Spengler's
extreme aim in mind: to explain the
very essence of mathematics as a social product, conditioned by and relative to socio-cultural systems and
historical epochs . . ." This paper
sketches "research in three areas:
(1) the social, economic, and political roots of mathematics in ancient
Greece and Europe; (2) continuities
and discontinuities in the development of mathematics in different

civilizations; and (3) patterns of
conflict and competition in the comparative history of mathematics."
This review of the authors' ongoing
work provides a glimpse of the issues and personalities occupying a
small but growing specialty, the
"sociology of mathematics."

S68. Dylander, Benny

    1980 "Technology Assessment--As Science
and as a Tool for Policy." Acta
Sociologica 23: 217-310.

S69. Latour, Bruno

    1980 "The Three Little Dinosaurs or a
Sociologists' Nightmare." Fundamen-
ta Scientiae 1: 79-85.
This "fable dedicated to the unknown
relativist" stars Realsaur, Scien-
taur, and Popsaur. It will either
amuse and fade or send the reader
scurrying for apparently more serious
versions of the argument contained
in chapter 4 of Latour and Woolgar
[L12] or the "constructivist" writings of Knorr [e.g., L08].

S70. van de Vall, Mark and Cheryl Bolas

    1980 "Applied Social Discipline Research
or Social Policy Research: The Emergence of a Professional Paradigm in
Sociological Research." The American Sociologist 15 (August): 128-
137.

S71. Demerath, N.J., III

    1980 "ASAing the Future: The Profession

vs. the Discipline?" <u>The American
Sociologist</u> 16 (May): 87-90.
An incisive look at intellectual
tensions and prospects.

S72.   Oromaner, Mark

1981 "Cognitive Consensus in Recent Mainstream American Sociology: An Empirical Analysis." <u>Scientometrics</u> 3
(March): 73-84.

S73.   Stehr, Nico

1981 "Sociological Languages." <u>Philosophy
of the Social Sciences</u> 11: forthcoming.
This paper argues that "a sociological analysis of the present state
of sociological languages and its
transformation is possible and necessary; . . . such an analysis . . .
should provide us with more adequate
insights into the conditions for the
possibility of certain forms of development of sociological knowledge."

S74.   Collins, H.M. and T.J. Pinch

1981 <u>Frames of Meaning: The Social Construction of Extraordinary Science</u>:
London: Routledge and Kegan Paul.

The complete case study of parapsychology and the process of "accom-
plishing objectivity."

LAB-CENTERED: A Laboratory Site or Local Organization
Focus Defines the Analysis

L01. Marcson, Simon

> 1972 "Research Settings." Pp. 161-191 in
> S.Z. Nagi and R.G. Corwin (eds.),
> The Social Contexts of Research.
> New York: Wiley-Interscience.

L02. Morrell, J.B.

> 1972 "The Chemist Breeders: The Research
> Laboratories of Liebig and Thomas
> Thomson." Ambix 19:1-46.
> "An examination of the factors af-
> fecting the success of two major ear-
> ly nineteenth century laboratories"
> [M].

L03. Whitley, R.D. and P. Frost

> 1972 "Authority, Problem-Solving Ap-
> proaches, Communication and Change
> in a British Research Laboratory."
> Journal of Management Studies 9: 337-
> 361.

L04. Whitley, Richard and P. Frost

> 1973 "Task Type and Information Transfer
> in a Government Research Lab." Hu-
> man Relations 25: 537-550.

L05. Bitz, A., A. McAlpine, and R.D. Whitley

> 1975 The Production, Flow and Use of In-
> formation in Research Laboratories
> in Different Sciences. Manchester:
> Manchester Business School.
> This report features a summary plus
> a dozen "appendices" on communication

184

patterns in high energy physics, geology, cancer research, and clinical
biomedical research in the U.K. "The
results suggest that most scientists
see their professional information
requirements in terms of immediate,
short-term activities and do not en-
gage in regular, frequent communication with other scientists." This
emphasis on the organization of local research groups is elaborated
in Whitley [L09].

L06.   Collins, H.M. and R.G. Harrison

1975   "Building a TEA Laser: The Caprices
of Communication." Social Studies
of Science 5: 441-450.
"[T]his account may be of interest
. . . as a partial description of
day-to-day laboratory activity, and
hence as an antidote to any too-easy
characterization of experimental replication as a 'routine' activity."
A useful elaboration on Collins
[P08].

L07.   Pelz, Donald C. and Frank M. Andrews

1976   Scientists in Organizations: Productive Climates for Research and Development. Revised Edition. Ann
Arbor, Mich.: Institute for Social
Research, University of Michigan.

This collection focuses on the authors' investigation of factors which
affect the performance of scientists
and engineers in R&D labs. These
studies of NASA teams as well as
medical sociologists underscore the
culture-, situation-, or work con-
text-specificity of individual per-

formance, irrespective of its measurement in terms of creativity (of
input), innovativeness (of output),
usefulness (to one's co-workers),
or leadership style. Unfortunately,
the content of the technical problems
researched in the lab escapes the
authors' approach.

L08. Knorr, Karin D.

1977 "Producing and Reproducing Knowledge:
Descriptive or Constructive?" Social Science Information 16: 669-
696.
A model of research production is
proposed, based on the author's study
of a Berkeley biochemistry (plant
protein) lab. The model emphasizes
"the idiosyncratic opportunities of
local research sites," and includes
discussions of "success," "constructive tinkering," and research "in-
vestments." This paper is a provi-
sional statement of the theory of
scientific practice contained in
Knorr [L11 , L25].

L09. Whitley, R.D.

1977 "The Sociology of Scientific Work
and the History of Scientific Developments." Pp. 21-50 in S.S. Blume
(ed.,), Perspectives in the Sociology of Science. Chichester: Wiley.

The author argues convincingly that
scientific organization constrains
both the form and content of intellectual work, and therefore, what
constitutes change within "restricted"
and "unrestricted" sciences. While
overextended, the argument succeeds

in putting the "local" back into the "local-cosmopolitan" continuum of scientists' organizational orientation and style.

L10.   Whitley, R.D.

1978   "Types of Science, Organizational Strategies and Patterns of Work in Research Laboratories in Different Scientific Fields." Social Science Information 17: 427-447.
. . . more of what can be found in Whitley [L09].

L11.   Knorr, K.D.

1979   "Tinkering Toward Success: Prelude to a Theory of Scientific Practice." Theory and Society 8: 347-376.

L12.   Latour, Bruno and Steve Woolgar

1979   Laboratory Life: The Social Construction of Scientific Facts. Beverly Hills: Sage.
This first book-length study, based on intense observation of a scientific laboratory, makes a strong and witty case for an anthropological or ethnographic approach to science. Whether describing the "credit cycle" of career contingencies or the renegotiation of empirical claims—concerning the isolation and identification of the chemical structure of Thyrotropin Releasing Factor (TRF)— the authors are refreshing, penetrating, and thoroughly debunking. Such in situ studies are destined to provide a foil for other approaches to specialization in science.

L12a.   Bazerman, Charles

1980   (Review).   4S Newsletter 5 (Spring):
       14-19.
       "Working from the data of Latour's
       two years' observation of daily ac-
       tivity in the Salk Institute for Bio-
       logical Studies, the two authors ex-
       plore how laboratory activities are
       transformed into published statements
       through . . . 'literary inscription,'
       and how those statements gain 'cre-
       dit' to emerge as accepted fact out
       of the many contending statements
       proposed in the literature of the
       field. . . . Once having taken the
       position that science is driven only
       by the dynamics of its construction
       . . . [the authors] are moved to show
       that scientific reality, constructed
       in daily conversation in the labora-
       tory, is the same as everyday reality,
       constructed in everyday conversation."

L12b.   Cozzens, Susan E.

1980   (Review).   4S Newsletter 5 (Spring):
       19-21.
       "I do not think that this book will
       be the programmatic statement of the
       [phenomenological] approach [to the
       social study of science] . . . it may
       turn out to be an exemplar, a conglo-
       meration of theory, method, and ob-
       servation which will form a rich
       source of insight, in a fuzzy way,
       for much future work. . . . Labora-
       tory Life ends up saying more about
       how to think about science than about
       how to study it, and even less about
       the character of science itself."

L13.   Tushman, Michael

       1979   "Technical Communication in Research
              and Development Laboratories: Impact
              of Project Work Characteristics."
              Academy of Management Journal 22:
              624-645.

L14.   Chubin, D.E. and T. Connolly

       1980   "Research Trails and Science Poli-
              cies: Local and Extra-Local Negotia-
              tion of Scientific Work." Presented
              at the Conference on Scientific Es-
              tablishments and Hierarchies, Oxford
              University (July) (Sociology of the
              Sciences, Vol. 6, forthcoming).

              The authors argue "that there exist
              important pressures which lead to
              undue persistence of individuals in
              some research trails rather than
              others; that the social processes
              associated with the development of
              these trails tend toward conservative
              pressures for intellectual continuity
              . . . . and that the aggregate result
              of these processes is that, far from
              a wide dispersion of research effort
              around the boundary problems of a spe-
              cialty, there will be unproductive
              over-concentration on some few pro-
              blems, while high-potential areas
              go underdeveloped."

L15.   Knorr, K.D., R. Krohn, and R. Whitley
       (eds.)

       1980   The Social Process of Scientific
              Investigation. Sociology of the
              Sciences, Vol. 4. Dordrecht: D.
              Reidel.
              This largely European collection

takes a giant step toward understanding the process of research production. Especially recommended are the papers on "discovery acceptance" by Pinch [P51], Pickering [P50], Harvey [P47], and Travis [B53], as well as those on "accounts" by Latour [L17] and Woolgar [G62].

L16. Knorr, Karin D.

1980 "Anthropology of Scientific Knowledge." Presented at the Conference on Science/Technology Studies, Toronto (October).
This review of five lab studies of scientific work focuses on five major issues. Collectively, according to the author, they suggest: (1) "the conception of knowledge production as constructive rather than descriptive; (2) the situated and contingent (circumstantial) character of the construction of scientific objects; (3) the motion of a radically participant-centered perspective (Edge [G51]) . . . in contrast to the established concept of scientific integration; (4) the literary and discursive nature of scientific activities and of the practical reasoning displayed in laboratory work; and (5) the question . . . of the recent distinction between the natural and the social sciences . . . [given] the evidence we now have about natural science inquiry."

L17. Latour, Bruno

1980 "Is It Possible to Reconstruct the Research Process? Sociology of a

190

Brain Peptide." Pp. 53-73 in K.D. Knorr et al. (eds.), [L15].
In one incisive quote, the author summarizes an approach and a program of research: "In the old framework, we had to observe scientists from the outside, to threaten them, or worse, to give up studying and pass inside their fortress to worship them or become their servants. Now that we are all equally inside the heterogeneous, opportunistic, fictional science that is built, new alliances are possible that are much more interesting than the boring 'tete-a-tete' of scientists and their observer." For details, see Latour [S69] and Latour and Woolgar [L12].

L18.   McKegney, Doug

1980   "Inquiry into Inquiry: Local Action and Public Discourse in Wild Life Ecology." Presented at the Conference on Science/Technology Studies, Toronto (October).
Sketches the author's experiences in a field-lab study of the reproductive ecology of deer (as part of his MSc thesis in preparation, Simon Fraser University).

L19.   Tushman, Michael L. and Ralph Katz

1980   "External Communication and Project Performance: An Investigation into the Role of Gatekeepers." Management Science 26: 1071-1085.
"This study investigates the role of gatekeepers in the transfer of information in a single R&D setting by comparing directly the performance

of project groups with and without gatekeepers." This recent management-oriented lab study provides a counterpoint to the anthropological approaches to research organization now emerging.

L20.   Zenzen, Michael and Sal Restivo

      1980   "The Mysterious Morphology of Immiscible Liquids: The Discovery and Pursuit of an Anomaly in Colloid Chemistry." Presented at the Conference on the Social Process of Scientific Investigation, McGill University.
             An account of scientific practice in a chemistry lab. The authors argue that "contingencies" are an integral part of laboratory work.

L21.   Anderson, Robert S.

      1981   "The Necessity of Field Methods in the Study of Scientific Research." Pp. 213-244 in E. Mendelsohn and Y. Elkana (eds.), Sciences and Cultures. Sociology of the Sciences, Vol. 5. Boston and Dordrecht: D. Reidel.
             An anthropologist discusses "the research institution as the mediator between 'the scientific tradition' and individual researchers' contributions to it, and national policies and socio-cultural systems."

L22.   Goodfield, June

      1981   An Imagined World: A Story of Scientific Discovery. New York: Harper and Row.

L22a. Pert, Candace

    1981 "Anna of the Spirits" (Review).
Science 81 (March): 101+.
The author "has managed to communicate Anna's ideas in the context of
contemporary immunology so dazzlingly
that the book is, I believe, a realistic rendition of what exceptional
scientists do with an idea when they
are obsessed by it and are strong
enough to nurture it in the face of
disbelief from other members of the
scientific community."

L22b. Shelanski, Vivien B.

    1981 "A Walk into Science." (Review).
Science, Technology, and Human Values
6 (Summer): 59-61.
Goodfield advocates that we "move
into the laboratory to observe and
try to penetrate the mind of the
scientist. . . . By adopting this
quasi-anthropological approach, [she]
hopes to provide a 'window' on one
individual's process of doing creative science." The individual is
"Anna Brito," a cancer researcher;the
process chronicled here lasts five
years, a period of Brito's "emergence
. . . as a leader of a laboratory
group. The alternating patterns of
lonely concentration and team endeav-
or stand out sharply from these
pages."

L23. Knorr, Karin

    1981 "The Ethnography of Laboratory Life:

Empirical Results and Theoretical
Challenges." International Society
for the Society of Knowledge Newsletter 7 (May): 4-9.
The author succinctly reviews five
major lab studies, offering a "constructivist interpretation of local
context and discourse analysis of
scientific practice. For fuller
treatments, see e.g., Knorr [L08 ,
L25], Lynch [L27], McKegney [L18],
and Zenzen and Restivo [L20].

L24.   Knorr, K.D.

1981   "Scientific Communities or Variable
Transscientific Fields? A Critique
of Quasi-Economic Models of Science."
Social Studies of Science 11: forthcoming.
This paper, informed by laboratory
observation, criticizes the notion
of specialty communities and of community-based, quasi-economic models
of science, and proposes a model of
the "transscientific" connections
of research, that is, "networks of
symbolic relationships which in
principle go beyond the boundaries
of a scientific community or scientific field . . ." Such a network
defines as relevant members some of
whom are neither specialists nor
scientists, such as program managers
of funding agencies.

L25.   Knorr, K.D.

1981   The Manufacture of Knowledge: An Essay
on the Constructivist and Contextual
Nature of Science.   Oxford: Pergamon.

194

L26.   Knorr, K.D. and D.W. Knorr

        1981   "From Scenes to Scripts: On the Re-
                lationship between Laboratory Re-
                search and Published Paper in Sci-
                ence." Social Studies of Science
                11 forthcoming .
                " . . . the origin and dynamics of
                a research effort in the laboratory
                are outlined and compared with the
                account given in the scientific pub-
                lication . . ." Strategies of per-
                suasion are examined by means of dis-
                course analysis, revealing that "a
                conception of the scientific paper
                as a 'relevant summary description'
                of what happened in the laboratory
                cannot be substantiated."

L27.   Lynch, Michael

        1981   Art and Artifact in Laboratory Sci-
                ence: A Study of Shop Work and Shop
                Talk in a Research Laboratory. Lon-
                don: Routledge and Kegan Paul.
                An ethnomethodological investigation
                of brain science research based on
                the author's Ph.D. dissertation (Uni-
                versity of California, Irvine, 1979).

L28.   Tilley, Nicholas

        1981   "The Logic of Laboratory Life."
                Sociology 15 (February): 117-126.
                A review article that focuses on La-
                tour and Woolgar [L12], arguing--
                surprise !--that the work as a whole
                "constitutes a striking corrobora-
                tion of the Popperian philosophy of
                science . . ."

L29. Traweek, Sharon

1981 "Culture and the Organization of
      the Particle Physics Communities in
      Japan and the United States." Pre-
      sented at the Conference on Communi-
      cation in Scientific Research, Simon
      Fraser University (September).
      A very readable journalistic account
      of "three intersecting cultures at
      work" in particle physics labora-
      tories: local, national, and (sub)
      disciplinary. The account is based
      on the anthropologist – author's
      nearly five years of observations at
      three labs (SLAC, Fermi-lab and KEK
      at Tsukuba).

L30. Woolgar, Steve

1981 "Science and Ethnomethodology: A
      Prefatory Statement." International
      Society for the Sociology of Know-
      ledge Newsletter 7 (May): 10-15.

      A schematic treatment of "concerns
      common to ethnomethodology and the
      social study of science." The au-
      thor's distinction of the ethnome-
      thodologist's task as "documenting
      the constructive work of their sub-
      jects" instead of "explaining" it
      is provocative indeed for the would-
      be ethnographer of science.

III. AUTHOR INDEX

Underlined letters and numbers refer
to pages in the Introduction (I) where
authors are cited. Other Letter-Num-
bers refer to entries in sections of
the Subject Classification.